Published in 2017 by Bounty Books based on materials licensed to it by Bauer Media Books, Australia.

Bauer Media Books

Publisher
Jo Runciman

Editorial & food director
Sophia Young

Director of sales, marketing & rights
Brian Cearnes

Editorial director-at-large
Pamela Clark

Creative director & designer
Hannah Blackmore

Managing editor
Stephanie Kistner

Senior food editor
Kathleen Davis

Junior editor
Amanda Lees

Operations manager
David Scotto

Printed in China
by Leo Paper Products Ltd.

Published and distributed in
the United Kingdom by Bounty Books,
a division of Octopus Publishing Group Ltd
Carmelite House
50 Victoria Embankment
London, EC4Y 0DZ
United Kingdom
info@octopus-publishing.co.uk;
www.octopusbooks.co.uk

International foreign language rights
Brian Cearnes, Bauer Media Books
bcearnes@bauer-media.com.au

A catalogue record for this book is
available from the British Library.

ISBN: 978-0-75373-262-5

© Bauer Media Pty Ltd 2017
ABN 18 053 273 546

The
Mediterranean
Diet

Bounty
BOOKS

Contents

Mediterranean Life

*The Mediterranean diet isn't a trend, fad or set of food rules.
It's a real food approach to healthy eating that embraces variety, flavour
and nutrient-rich foods. The diet, which is often referred to as the
world's healthiest diet, is backed by plenty of scientific evidence showing
that people who eat a Mediterranean diet tend to live long and healthy lives.*

It's no longer a secret that people who eat a Mediterranean diet share many commonalities including a longer life expectancy, healthier hearts and lower rates of chronic disease. The positive effects of the diet are far reaching and include lower levels of 'bad' LDL cholesterol, better blood glucose (sugar) control, better weight management, reduced risk of depression, as well as a lower incidence of some cancers, Parkinson's and Alzheimer's diseases.

The Mediterranean diet is centered on real, minimally processed foods such as wholegrains, plenty of plant foods such as fruit and vegetables, as well as seafood and fish, yoghurt, pulses, seeds and nuts. There is no need to give up your favourite foods, as the Mediterranean diet includes many of them, such as red wine, extra virgin olive oil, butter and bread. Ultimately, balance and enjoyment are at the core of the Mediterranean approach to food.

Cutting out fat isn't encouraged on a Mediterranean diet. When it comes to good nutrition, not all fats are created equal. In fact, research suggests that including healthy fats as part of a healthy, balanced diet can actually promote better health outcomes and may be the reason why people who follow a Mediterranean diet have healthier hearts than those who eat a traditional Western diet.

Healthy fats including extra virgin olive oil, nuts and seeds, oily fish and dairy foods like yoghurt are all included on the Mediterranean menu. Extra virgin olive oil features as the primary source of fat in the Mediterranean diet – and not just because it tastes great. Olive oil is a really good source of monounsaturated fat, which has been linked with lower levels of 'bad' LDL cholesterol and heart disease and better weight management. Olive oil also contains linoleic acid, a type of

omega-6 fatty acid, which is good news for your heart. Where possible, opt for extra virgin olive oil as your primary source of fat. In particular, choose "extra virgin" and "virgin" options, as these are the least processed whilst containing the highest levels of beneficial polyphenols, the protective compound found in plants.

Instead of cutting out fat altogether, with the Mediterranean diet you simply swap sources of saturated and trans fats for foods with more monounsaturated and polyunsaturated fats. Choose foods like avocado, nuts, seeds, oily fish, extra virgin olive oil and dairy foods rather than filling up on too much red meat or deep-fried and processed options.

Seafood and fish also feature heavily in the Mediterranean kitchen, offering a healthier and more sustainable alternative to red meat. Oily fish, such as sardines, herring, tuna, salmon, mackerel, are all

good sources of heart-healthy omega-3 fatty acids, a polyunsaturated fat which research suggests can help boost brain function including memory, concentration and mood.

Whilst small amounts of meat can be eaten in the diet, seafood and fish are at the heart of the Mediterranean diet, along with plant-based sources of protein such as pulses, nuts and seeds. Aim to eat fish or seafood at least twice a week and ideally eat a small serve of red meat two or three times a week.

The Mediterranean diet also features plenty of unrefined wholegrains and other fibre-rich foods such as vegetables and fruit. This plant-based focus is a great way to get lots of fibre into your diet, fueling your body with naturally slow burning energy sources. A diet high in fibre is linked to better weight management and digestion, improved cholesterol levels, reduced risk of some

diseases including bowel cancer, as well as more stable moods. Get inspiration from the Mediterranean way of eating and choose wholegrains such as oats, brown and black rice, quinoa, freekeh and barley over more refined options. Adding legumes or pulses into your diet is also a great way to up your fibre intake – and stay fuller for longer.

Many of the Mediterranean-style dishes are naturally bright and colourful, thanks to the importance placed on fresh, seasonal produce. Fruit and vegetables naturally contain plenty of antioxidants and polyphenols, which can help combat free radical damage helping to slow the signs of ageing and reduce the risk of inflammatory disease. Filling up on five to ten serves of vegetables a day is a great way to get more antioxidants, polyphenols, vitamins, minerals and fibre into your diet. But it's not just the type of foods consumed in the Mediterranean that

makes it so good for you. It is the way in which the food is eaten, with importance placed on meal times, which is also a critical factor.

Most Mediterranean dishes are designed to be enjoyed with family and friends. This family-style approach to eating food around the table helps develop a sense of community and connection that is essential to wellbeing and happiness. Sharing foods around the table also helps foster a healthy relationship with food where the focus is on enjoyment and satiation, rather than restriction or control. Eating at the table is a simple step that can promote more mindfulness into meal times.

Another benefit of eating family-style share plates is that it encourages a diet of variety. Variety is at the core of the Mediterranean diet. Eating a diet that includes a wide range of ingredients, in an array of colours is a simple way to help

your body get a healthy mix of essential vitamins and minerals. Get more variety in your diet by 'eating the rainbow', choosing mostly plant foods and trying new ingredients, particularly as the seasons change. Naturally, you'll fill up on more nutrient-rich foods helping your body to thrive.

The Mediterranean diet is easy to follow because there are no food rules or lists of banned foods. Instead of counting kilojoules, a Mediterranean approach can help you take care of your body by simply tuning into your appetite, eating when hungry and filling up on plenty of the good stuff. Ultimately, the Mediterranean diet is an enjoyable, easy-to-adopt way of eating to help you live a longer, healthier and happier life filled with energy, balance and shared experiences eating together.

Lyndi Cohen, The Nude Nutritionist
Accredited Practising Dietitian & Nutritionist
www.lyndicohen.com

Breakfast & Light Meals

pearl barley & cherry breakfast bowl

SERVES 2

One of the first cultivated grains in history, barley is a wonderfully versatile wholegrain, with a rich nutty flavour, packed with fibre. Here we have used it to make a sweet breakfast bowl, but it can also be used to bulk out a vegetable soup or in place of red meat in a hearty, winter stew. Sheeps' milk yoghurt can be purchased from health food stores and some supermarkets.

TIPS You could also try this with cooked quinoa instead of barley. Frozen raspberries can be used instead of cherries. Use fresh pitted cherries when in season.

DO-AHEAD
This recipe can be prepared the day before up to the end of step 1.

PREP + COOK TIME 50 MINUTES

½ CUP (100G) PEARL BARLEY

1½ CUPS (375ML) WATER

1 CUP (280G) SHEEP'S MILK YOGHURT

½ TEASPOON GROUND CINNAMON

1½ CUPS (185G) FROZEN PITTED CHERRIES,
   THAWED, HALVED

30G (1 OUNCE) FRESH HONEYCOMB, SLICED

2 TABLESPOONS COARSELY CHOPPED
   NATURAL ALMONDS

GROUND CINNAMON, EXTRA, TO SERVE

1 Place barley and the water in a small saucepan, bring to the boil. Reduce heat to low; cook, covered, for 35 minutes or until tender. Drain. Rinse under cold water until cool; drain well.

2 Combine barley, yoghurt, cinnamon and ⅔ cup of cherries in a medium bowl. Divide between two bowls. Top with remaining cherries, the honeycomb and almonds; dust with extra ground cinnamon.

omelette with asparagus & mint

MAKES 2

This omelette is studded with the traditional flavours of spring – asparagus, peas and fresh herbs. Eating what is in season is a fundamental part of the Mediterranean diet, as produce will never be as flavoursome or nutrient-rich as when grown in its correct season. Eggs are a great source of protein, keeping you fuller for longer, making them the perfect way to start your day.

TIP You can swap asparagus for broccolini, if you like.

PREP + COOK TIME 20 MINUTES

200G (6 ½ OUNCES) POTATO,

CUT INTO 5MM (¼-INCH) CUBES

170G (5½ OUNCES) ASPARAGUS, TRIMMED

1 CUP (120G) FROZEN PEAS

4 EGGS

⅓ CUP COARSELY CHOPPED FRESH MINT LEAVES

1½ TABLESPOONS EXTRA VIRGIN OLIVE OIL

SOURDOUGH BREAD, TOASTED, TO SERVE

1 Cook potato in a small saucepan of boiling water for 3 minutes. Add asparagus and peas; cook a further 1 minute or until asparagus is bright green and potato is tender. Drain. When cool enough to handle, cut the asparagus in half; thinly slice the stem ends crossways.

2 Lightly whisk eggs in a medium bowl; stir in potato, mint, half the peas and the chopped asparagus ends.

3 Heat half the oil in a small non-stick frying pan over high heat; cook half the egg mixture for 2 minutes, pulling in the egg with a spatula to help it cook quickly. Fold one side of the omelette over using the spatula; slide onto a warm plate. Repeat with remaining oil and egg mixture to make second omelette. Season.

4 Top omelettes with remaining asparagus and peas; serve with toasted sourdough. Sprinkle with extra mint leaves, if you like.

pumpkin fatteh with almond skordalia

SERVES 4

Fatteh is an Arabic word meaning 'crushed' or 'crumbs'. In a recipe it refers to fresh or toasted flat breads covered with other ingredients, such as the vegetables in this salad. You could make extra and use as an accompaniment to dip or salsa for a healthy snack, or starter for a shared meal.

DO-AHEAD You can assemble the salad ahead of time, omitting the bread. Serve bread on the salad, or on the side.

PREP + COOK TIME 45 MINUTES

800G (1½-POUND) SMALL KENT PUMPKIN, CUT INTO THIN WEDGES

¼ CUP (60ML) EXTRA VIRGIN OLIVE OIL

1½ TABLESPOONS ZA'ATAR

2 MEDIUM RED CAPSICUMS (BELL PEPPERS) (400G), SLICED THICKLY

1 MEDIUM RED ONION (170G), SLICED THICKLY

1 LARGE WHOLEMEAL LEBANESE BREAD ROUND (100G), SPLIT INTO TWO ROUNDS

300G (9½ OUNCES) CANNED CHICKPEAS (GARBANZO BEANS), DRAINED, RINSED

2 TABLESPOONS PINE NUTS, TOASTED

⅓ CUP FRESH FLAT-LEAF PARSLEY LEAVES

⅓ CUP FRESH MINT LEAVES

LEMON WEDGES, TO SERVE

ALMOND SKORDALIA

1 CUP (160G) BLANCHED ALMONDS

2 CLOVES GARLIC, CRUSHED

1 CUP (70G) COARSELY CHOPPED DAY-OLD BREAD

2 TABLESPOONS WHITE WINE VINEGAR

⅓ CUP (80ML) EXTRA VIRGIN OLIVE OIL

½ CUP (125ML) WATER

1 Preheat oven to 220°C/425°F. Line two large oven trays with baking paper.

2 Place pumpkin wedges on one tray; drizzle with 1 tablespoon of the oil and sprinkle with 1 tablespoon of the za'atar; season. Roast for 30 minutes or until just tender. Meanwhile, place capsicum and onion on second tray; drizzle with another tablespoon of the oil. Season; roast for 20 minutes or until tender.

3 Place bread on a third unlined oven tray, lightly brush with remaining oil; season. Toast bread for 3 minutes or until crisp; cool. Break into pieces.

4 Make almond skordalia.

5 Place vegetables, chickpeas, pine nuts, parsley and mint on a platter; top with remaining za'atar. Serve with almond skordalia, toasted bread and lemon wedges.

ALMOND SKORDALIA Place almonds in a heavy-based frying pan; stir constantly over medium to high heat until they are browned evenly. Remove from pan; cool. Process almonds, garlic, bread and vinegar until wet breadcrumbs form. With motor operating, gradually add oil in a thin, steady stream; add the water, process until mixture is smooth. Season to taste.

grilled vegetable & ricotta bruschetta

SERVES 4

We all know bruschetta, the grilled bread anitipasto (starter) that is synonymous with Italian cuisine. Using stale bread, bruschetta brings new life to something that might otherwise be discarded, the toasted bread topped with a myriad of delicious ingredients, from beans and cured meats, to the recognisable tomato and garlic mixture of your local Italian restaurant.

TIPS Double the ricotta mixture and refrigerate half in an airtight container for up to 2 days to spread on toast or sandwiches or eat with crudités as a snack.

SERVING SUGGESTION Serve the bruschetta topped with a poached egg, if you like.

PREP + COOK TIME 30 MINUTES

2 TEASPOONS BALSAMIC VINEGAR

2 TABLESPOONS EXTRA VIRGIN OLIVE OIL

2 MEDIUM ZUCCHINI (240G), SLICED THINLY LENGTHWAYS

2 MEDIUM YELLOW CAPSICUM (BELL PEPPER) (200G), SLICED THICKLY

2 MEDIUM TOMATOES (300G), HALVED

4 LARGE SLICES SOURDOUGH BREAD (280G)

OLIVE-OIL SPRAY

1 CUP (240G) FRESH RICOTTA

1 TABLESPOON FINELY CHOPPED BASIL

2 TABLESPOONS SMALL FRESH BASIL LEAVES

60G (2 OUNCES) BABY ROCKET (ARUGULA) LEAVES

1 For the dressing, combine balsamic vinegar and 1 tablespoon of the oil in a small bowl.

2 Lightly spray zucchini, capsicum, tomato and bread with oil; season vegetables. Cook vegetables and bread, in batches, on a heated grill plate or barbecue until vegetables are tender and bread is lightly charred.

3 Place ricotta, chopped basil and remaining oil in a small bowl; stir to combine. Season to taste.

4 Spread ricotta mixture over toasted bread slices; top with vegetables and rocket. Drizzle with dressing and sprinkle with basil leaves.

The Greek diet

Greece, with its 4,000-year old cuisine, is arguably the original home of the Mediterranean diet. Like other Mediterranean countries, cooking here is regionally diverse but shares common ingredients and principles. Over the years, islands like Ikaria and Crete have captured the attention of researchers and those in search of a healthier diet. In these places residents live rich, long lives, many making it to 100 years and beyond. Not only that, they enjoy lower rates of diseases that plague modern life; Alzheimer's, certain cancers, heart disease and obesity. It's part of what's known as The Blue Zone, which refers to places in the world that are proven pockets of longevity and where people are, in general, healthier.

Ikaria, a 10-hour ferry-ride from Athens, is particularly isolated from the stresses of the modern world. The lifestyle here is inclusive and community-focused and convenience foods are largely unknown. Exercise and gardening are part of the typical daily routine and many of the vegetables that form the basis of their diet are home grown. A typical breakfast might be goat's milk yoghurt with herb tea or coffee and perhaps some wholegrain bread with raw honey. Drinking wine in the morning is not unknown! (Interestingly, Ikarians drink two to four glasses of wine a day and up to three cups of coffee a day. And the way they prepare their coffee, by boiling the grounds, has been shown to promote blood circulation.) Lunch might be a dish of vegetables like green beans, legumes, potatoes and perhaps some fresh-caught fish, cooked in liberal amounts of local olive oil. The evening meal tends to be light; wholegrain bread and more vegetables or a substantial salad. The little meat the islanders eat, usually pork, is home-raised. Most households process just one pig a year and serve the meat in small portions, saving it for special occasions. Afternoon napping, which scientists have shown can greatly reduce the risk of heart disease, is a regular practice.

As with the rest of Greece, lemon and fresh herbs are used widely to flavour meats, grains and vegetables. Lemons are not only full of vitamin C, but also increases iron absorption when consumed with iron-rich foods like meat and dried beans. Herbs, used in drinks as well as in cooking, are particularly potent, containing protective compounds that can be effective for everything from improving digestion and memory, to fighting colds. Oregano, which is often cooked with meat, contains antioxidants that can cancel out certain cancer-causing substances in red meat. Greeks love horta, a blanket term for flavoursome mixed greens, often foraged wild. Rich in antioxidants and minerals, they include amaranth, dandelion greens, mustard greens and chicory; used famously in spanakopita. Grape vine leaves, used as a wrapping for dolmades, have a potent nutritional profile, full of vitamins and minerals. They're also a powerful anti-inflammatory.

Seafood is a key ingredient; small fish like red mullet and sardines, plus octopus, are favourites. Sardines contain one of the highest levels of omega-3 of all fish, and octopus is rich in selenium. The range of fresh produce and quality ingredients used in Greek cooking is vast and can best be seen in mezedes, a snack-like course not unlike Spanish tapas.

THE GREEK LIFESTYLE

FETTA & YOGHURT
Eaten sparingly but often, these dairy products are iconic Greek staples. Tangy and fresh, sheep and goat's milk fetta is lower in fat than other cheeses and packed with nutrients.

FISH & SEAFOOD
Small fish rich in omega-3, such as red mullet and sardines, as well as octopus, are favourites.

DRIED BEANS & LEGUMES
Broad beans, split peas, chickpeas and lentils are staple, non-meat protein sources used in soups, stews and salads.

VEGETABLES
Many dishes, even main courses, are often comprised of vegetables, cooked simply in olive oil with plenty of herbs and garlic.

DESSERT
Usually comprised of fresh fruit or spoon sweets (fruits preserved in sugar), served with coffee.

GREEK HONEY
Ikarian islanders claim their legendary wild pine honey is a key to their longevity.

NUTS
Pine nuts, walnuts, almonds and chestnuts are all incorporated into many Greek regional dishes.

chickpea pancake with fried eggs & cherry tomatoes

SERVES 4

This chickpea pancake is very similar to socca, the traditional street food of Nice, or farinata, a baked chickpea pancake from Italy. Chickpea flour, also known as besan, is rich in protein and fibre, making it a nutritious and filling choice for breakfast. It is also completely gluten-free, so is a perfect healthy option for those who are sensitive or intolerant to gluten.

TIPS Chickpea flour (besan) is available from supermarkets and health food stores. Pancake is best made just before serving.

PREP + COOK TIME 30 MINUTES (+ COOLING)

⅔ CUP (100G) CHICKPEA FLOUR (BESAN)

1 TEASPOON GROUND CUMIN

½ TEASPOON SEA SALT FLAKES

¾ CUP (180ML) WATER

2 TABLESPOONS EXTRA VIRGIN OLIVE OIL

1 EGG WHITE

170G (5½ OUNCES) ASPARAGUS, TRIMMED

1 CLOVE GARLIC, CRUSHED

250G (8 OUNCES) MIXED CHERRY TOMATOES, HALVED

1 TABLESPOON RED WINE VINEGAR

4 EGGS

1 Preheat oven to 180°C/350°F.

2 Combine chickpea flour, cumin and salt in a medium bowl; season. Whisk in the water and 1 tablespoon of the oil until smooth.

3 Beat egg white in a bowl with an electric mixer until soft peaks form; fold into batter.

4 Heat an oiled 24cm (9½-inch) ovenproof non-stick frying pan over medium heat. Pour batter into pan; cook for 2 minutes or until bubbles form around the edge. Transfer pan to oven; cook for 7 minutes or until pancake is cooked through, and is light and fluffy.

5 Meanwhile, heat 2 teaspoons of the oil in a large non-stick frying pan over medium heat; cook asparagus for 5 minutes, turning, until lightly browned and tender. Remove from pan; keep warm.

6 Add garlic to same pan; cook, stirring, for 30 seconds or until fragrant. Add tomatoes and vinegar; cook, breaking tomatoes with the back of a wooden spoon, for 5 minutes or until tomatoes have just broken down. Season. Remove from pan; keep warm. Wipe pan clean with paper towel.

7 Heat remaining oil in same pan over medium heat. Add eggs; cook for 4 minutes or until whites are set and yolks remain runny, or cooked to your liking.

8 Cut pancake into wedges. Serve pancake with fried egg, tomato mixture and asparagus; season.

spiced couscous with passionfruit yoghurt

SERVES 4

Couscous consists of steamed balls of crushed durum wheat semolina, with a similar nutritional value of pasta (although pasta is more refined). Originally a North African dish, it travelled to the Mediterranean in the 17th century, and is now widely eaten in the region. It is particularly popular in France, but is also common in Spain, Portugal, Italy and Greece.

TIP Swap the blueberries for strawberries or raspberries, or use a mixture of all three, if you like.

PREP + COOK TIME 25 MINUTES

1 CUP (200G) WHOLEMEAL COUSCOUS

2 TEASPOONS EXTRA VIRGIN OLIVE OIL

1 TEASPOON MIXED SPICE

¼ TEASPOON ALLSPICE

¼ CUP (90G) HONEY

1 CUP (250ML) BOILING WATER

½ CUP (50G) WALNUTS, ROASTED

¾ CUP (200G) GREEK-STYLE YOGHURT

2 TABLESPOONS FRESH PASSIONFRUIT PULP

2 MEDIUM ORANGES (480G)

⅓ CUP (50G) BLUEBERRIES

2 TABLESPOONS FRESH MINT LEAVES

1 Combine couscous, oil, mixed spice, allspice, a pinch of salt and honey with the boiling water in a medium bowl. Stand, covered, for 5 minutes or until liquid is absorbed. Fluff with a fork. Stir in walnuts.

2 Meanwhile, combine yoghurt and passionfruit in a small bowl.

3 Finely grate the rind from one orange; you will need 1 teaspoon. Peel oranges, then thinly slice. Serve spiced couscous topped with orange slices, blueberries, passionfruit yoghurt, mint and rind.

cumin-baked beans

SERVES 6

Beans are a great vegetarian option that are packed with protein and fibre. Dried beans give a better flavour and texture than canned, though canned beans will work fine in this recipes. See Tips for the quantity of canned beans needed. Take leftover baked beans to work and reheat in the microwave for a delicious breakfast that has none of the added sugar or salt of the canned supermarket version.

TIPS To save time, use 3 x 400g cans drained and rinsed cannellini beans, instead of soaking dried beans. Sprinkle with fresh oregano leaves before serving, if you like.

PREP + COOK TIME 1 HOUR 20 MINUTES (+ OVERNIGHT SOAKING)

YOU WILL NEED TO START THIS RECIPE THE DAY BEFORE.

400G (12½ OUNCES) DRIED WHITE BEANS

2 TABLESPOONS EXTRA VIRGIN OLIVE OIL

2 MEDIUM ONIONS (300G), CHOPPED FINELY

8 CLOVES GARLIC, SLICED THINLY

1 TEASPOON GROUND CUMIN

2 FRESH LONG RED CHILLIES, SLICED THINLY

¼ CUP (70G) TOMATO PASTE

3 LARGE TOMATOES (660G), CHOPPED COARSELY

3 CUPS (750ML) VEGETABLE STOCK

2 TABLESPOONS COARSELY CHOPPED
   FRESH OREGANO

SOURDOUGH BREAD SLICES, GRILLED, TO SERVE

1 Place beans in a large bowl, cover with cold water; stand overnight. Drain. Rinse under cold water; drain.

2 Place beans in a medium saucepan, cover with water; bring to the boil over high heat. Boil for 30 minutes or until beans are almost tender. Drain.

3 Heat oil in a large heavy-based saucepan over medium heat. Add onion, garlic, cumin and chilli; cook, stirring occasionally, for 7 minutes or until onion is golden. Add paste, tomato and stock; bring to the boil. Reduce heat to medium, cook, covered, for 10 minutes or until sauce thickens slightly.

4 Add beans to pan; cook, covered, stirring occasionally, for 10 minutes. Remove lid; cook for 10 minutes or until beans are tender. Stir in chopped oregano; season to taste.

5 Serve cumin-baked beans with grilled bread.

spring greens & fetta bruschetta

SERVES 4

Pesto alla genovese is a sauce originating in Genoa, the capital city of Liguria, Italy. It is traditionally made by pounding or grinding garlic cloves, pine nuts, basil, cheese and olive oil together using a mortar and pestle. Today there are many variations of pesto from this one in our recipe which uses rocket and almonds, to others that use other fresh green herbs or even spinach or kale.

TIPS If fresh broad beans are in season, you could use 575g (1 pound) fresh broad (fava) beans in the pod instead of frozen. Leftover pesto can be served with grilled fish or chicken or tossed through hot pasta. Serving-sized portions of pesto can be frozen in small tightly-sealed containers for up to 3 months.

PREP + COOK TIME 40 MINUTES

1 CUP (150G) FROZEN BROAD (FAVA) BEANS, THAWED (SEE TIPS)

170G (5½ OUNCES) ASPARAGUS, TRIMMED, SLICED DIAGONALLY

½ CUP (60G) FROZEN PEAS

8 SLICES SOURDOUGH BREAD (280G)

1 TABLESPOON EXTRA VIRGIN OLIVE OIL

1 CLOVE GARLIC, CRUSHED

1 TABLESPOON LEMON JUICE

90G (3 OUNCES) DRAINED MARINATED FETTA, CRUMBLED

2 TABLESPOONS SMALL FRESH MINT LEAVES

1 TEASPOON FINELY GRATED LEMON RIND

ROCKET & ALMOND PESTO

60G (2 OUNCES) ROCKET (ARUGULA)

1 CUP FIRMLY PACKED FRESH BASIL LEAVES

½ CUP (70G) SLIVERED ALMONDS, ROASTED

1 CLOVE GARLIC, CRUSHED

1 TEASPOON FINELY GRATED LEMON RIND

⅓ CUP (25G) FINELY GRATED PARMESAN

½ CUP (125ML) EXTRA VIRGIN OLIVE OIL

1 Cook broad beans and asparagus in a medium saucepan of boiling water for 2 minutes. Add peas, cook for 2 minutes; drain. Refresh in a bowl of iced water; drain. Remove grey skins from broad beans.

2 Make rocket and almond pesto.

3 Cook bread on a heated oiled grill plate (or pan or barbecue) for 1 minute on each side or until lightly charred. Spread ⅓ cup pesto on the bread slices.

4 Heat oil in a medium frying pan over medium-high heat. Cook garlic for 1 minute. Add asparagus, beans and peas; cook for 1 minute or until hot. Stir in juice; season to taste.

5 Spoon vegetable mixture onto toasted bread; top with fetta, mint and rind.

ROCKET & ALMOND PESTO Process rocket, basil, almonds, garlic, lemon rind, parmesan and 1 tablespoon of the oil until coarsely chopped. With motor operating, add remaining oil in a thin, steady stream until mixture is smooth; season to taste. (Makes 1 cup)

baby beetroot, lentil & watercress salad

SERVES 4

French-style green lentils are closely related to the famous French lentils du puy; these green-blue, tiny lentils have a nutty, earthy flavour and a hardy nature that allows them to be rapidly cooked without disintegrating. Because they hold their shape better than ordinary lentils, they are perfect for a hearty salad, and make a great addition to soups and stews.

TIP To remove the seeds from the pomegranate, cut in half crossways; hold a half, cut-side down, in the palm of your hand over a small bowl, then hit the outside firmly with a wooden spoon. The seeds should fall out easily; discard any white pith that falls out with them. Repeat with the other half.

PREP + COOK TIME 40 MINUTES

1KG (2 POUNDS) BABY BEETROOT (BEETS), STEMS AND LEAVES ATTACHED

2 CLOVES GARLIC, SLICED

¼ CUP FRESH ROSEMARY LEAVES

2 TABLESPOONS EXTRA VIRGIN OLIVE OIL

¼ CUP (60ML) BALSAMIC VINEGAR

½ CUP (100G) DRIED FRENCH-STYLE GREEN LENTILS, RINSED

3 CUPS (90G) TRIMMED WATERCRESS

1 LARGE POMEGRANATE (430G), SEEDS REMOVED (SEE TIP)

⅓ CUP (45G) ROASTED HAZELNUTS, HALVED

1 Preheat oven to 200°C/400°F.

2 Trim beetroot tops to 4cm (1½ inches); reserve a few small leaves. Halve beetroot, or quarter if large. Place beetroot, garlic and rosemary in a large ovenproof dish; drizzle with oil and vinegar. Roast for 30 minutes or until tender.

3 Meanwhile, place lentils in a medium saucepan; cover with water. Bring to the boil; cook lentils for 25 minutes or until tender. Drain; rinse under cold water, drain.

4 Place lentils, roast beetroot and cooking juices, watercress, half the pomegranate seeds and half the hazelnuts in a large bowl; toss gently to combine. Season to taste.

5 Transfer to a large bowl or platter; top with remaining pomegranate seeds and hazelnuts, and reserved beetroot leaves.

roasted mushrooms with spinach, tomato & ricotta

SERVES 2

Ricotta is a soft, sweet, moist, cow-milk cheese with a low fat content (8.5%) and a slightly grainy texture. The name roughly translates as 'cooked again' and refers to ricotta's manufacture from a whey that is itself a by-product of other cheese making. Ricotta has been made on the Italian peninsula for centuries and has a special place in Italian cuisine. It is used in both sweet and savoury dishes.

TIP If baby vine-ripened truss tomatoes are not available, use cherry or baby roma (egg) tomatoes instead.

PREP + COOK TIME 40 MINUTES

4 LARGE FLAT MUSHROOMS (400G), TRIMMED

275G (9 OUNCES) BABY VINE-RIPENED

   TRUSS TOMATOES

2 TABLESPOONS EXTRA VIRGIN OLIVE OIL

2 CLOVES GARLIC, CRUSHED

1 TABLESPOON BALSAMIC VINEGAR

12 SPRIGS FRESH THYME

50G (1½ OUNCES) BABY SPINACH LEAVES

¼ CUP (25G) FRESH RICOTTA, CRUMBLED

SOURDOUGH BREAD SLICES, TOASTED, TO SERVE

1 Preheat oven to 200°C/400°F. Line a large roasting pan with baking paper.

2 Place mushrooms and tomato in lined pan; drizzle evenly with half the oil. Season.

3 Combine garlic, vinegar and remaining oil in a small bowl; drizzle over mushrooms, then sprinkle with thyme. Cover pan loosely with baking paper; bake for 20 minutes.

4 Discard top baking paper. Tuck spinach leaves under mushrooms and tomato. Top mushrooms with ricotta. Bake for 5 minutes or until vegetables are tender. Serve with toasted sourdough.

glazed fig bruschetta

SERVES 4

Figs are one of the most recognisable Mediterranean fruits, featuring heavily in the art and myths of the region. In fact, figs are thought to be the first fruit to be cultivated by humans for food, and were widely consumed in ancient Greece and Rome. Try to use local honey for this recipe, which has a stronger and more flavoursome taste than commercial honey that has been highly refined.

TIP You can swap chopped pistachios or flaked almonds for the walnuts, if you like.

PREP + COOK TIME 10 MINUTES

6 MEDIUM FIGS (360G), HALVED

⅓ CUP (115G) HONEY

2 TABLESPOONS COLD WATER

⅔ CUP (190G) GREEK-STYLE YOGHURT

⅓ CUP (85G) MASCARPONE

1 TABLESPOON ICING (CONFECTIONERS') SUGAR

4 THICK SLICES SOURDOUGH BREAD (280G),
   TOASTED

2 TABLESPOONS COARSELY CHOPPED WALNUTS
   (SEE TIP)

1 Heat a large non-stick frying pan over medium-high heat. Drizzle cut-sides of figs with honey. Cook figs, cut-side down, for 2 minutes or until figs are glazed and warmed through. Add the water to pan; remove from heat.

2 Meanwhile, whisk yoghurt, mascarpone and sifted icing sugar in a small bowl until combined.

3 Spread toast evenly with mascarpone mixture; top with figs and walnuts. Before serving, drizzle with cooking juices.

gazpacho with fetta & prawns

SERVES 6

TIP Use the ripest tomatoes you can find to maximise the flavour of this classic Spanish soup.

PREP + COOK TIME 20 MINUTES

8 MEDIUM TOMATOES (1.2KG), CHOPPED COARSELY

2 MEDIUM RED CAPSICUMS (BELL PEPPER) (400G),
  CHOPPED COARSELY

2 LEBANESE CUCUMBERS (260G), PEELED,
  CHOPPED COARSELY

1 SMALL ONION (80G), CHOPPED COARSELY

3 CLOVES GARLIC, CRUSHED

160G (5 OUNCES) SOURDOUGH BREAD,
  CHOPPED COARSELY

1¼ CUPS (310ML) EXTRA VIRGIN OLIVE OIL

½ CUP (125ML) RED WINE VINEGAR

1 CUP (250ML) WATER

1KG (2 POUNDS) COOKED MEDIUM KING PRAWNS
  (SHRIMP)

4 SLICES SOURDOUGH BREAD (200G), EXTRA,
  CRUSTS REMOVED

160G (5 OUNCES) GREEK FETTA, CRUMBLED

2 TABLESPOONS SMALL FRESH OREGANO LEAVES

1 Blend tomato, capsicum, cucumber, onion, garlic, bread, 1 cup of the oil, the vinegar and the water for 3 minutes or until smooth. Season to taste.

2 Shell and devein prawns, leaving tails intact.

3 Tear extra sourdough into coarse pieces. Heat 2 tablespoons of the oil in a large frying pan over medium-high heat. Cook bread, stirring frequently, for 2 minutes or until croûtons are golden.

4 Ladle soup into serving bowls; top with croûtons, fetta, prawns and oregano leaves. Drizzle soup with remaining oil.

pan con tomate

SERVES 2

Pan con tomate is a staple breakfast in Spain and is a humble dish full of robust flavours. The key to its simplicity is to have summer-ripe tomatoes, good-quality bread and delicious olive oil. You could serve this as a starter at a party, or pair with a hearty salad for a light summer dinner.

TIP If truss cherry tomatoes are unavailable, use regular cherry or grape tomatoes instead.

SERVING SUGGESTION If you can't go past eggs at breakfast time, serve topped with a fried or soft-boiled egg.

PREP + COOK TIME 15 MINUTES

500G (1 POUND) BABY TRUSS CHERRY TOMATOES

¼ CUP (60ML) EXTRA VIRGIN OLIVE OIL

4 LARGE SLICES SOURDOUGH BREAD (240G)

1 CLOVE GARLIC, HALVED

70G (2½ OUNCES) GOAT'S CHEESE, CRUMBLED

2 TABLESPOONS FRESH OREGANO LEAVES

1 Preheat oven to 200°C/400°F. Line an oven tray with baking paper.

2 Place tomatoes on tray, drizzle with 2 tablespoons oil; season. Roast for 10 minutes or until skins burst and tomatoes have softened.

3 Drizzle bread with remaining oil. Cook on a heated grill plate (or barbecue) for 1 minute each side or until lightly charred. Rub grilled bread slices with the cut side of the garlic.

4 Squash warm tomatoes onto the toasted bread slices. Top with cheese and oregano.

green minestrone with pesto

SERVES 4

There is no set recipe for minestrone, traditionally made with whatever vegetables are in season at the time of cooking. Commonly the soup contains borlotti beans, but ours instead uses cannellini beans and substitutes tomato for freshly made pesto and bright green vegetables.

TIP Cut the leek in half lengthways and rinse carefully between the layers; they can be gritty.

DO-AHEAD Soup can be made a day ahead; keep covered in the fridge. Pesto can be made 3 days ahead; keep tightly covered, in a small airtight container, in the fridge. Soup and pesto can be frozen separately, for up to 3 months.

PREP + COOK TIME 35 MINUTES

2 TABLESPOONS EXTRA VIRGIN OLIVE OIL

1 TEASPOON FINELY CHOPPED FRESH SAGE LEAVES

2 CLOVES GARLIC, CHOPPED FINELY

1 MEDIUM LEEK (350G), CHOPPED FINELY

1 MEDIUM PARSNIP (250G), CUT INTO
   1CM (½-INCH) CUBES

2 TRIMMED CELERY STALKS (200G), SLICED THINLY

150G (4½ OUNCES) CURLY KALE, STEMS DISCARDED,
   TORN INTO PIECES

1.5 LITRES (6 CUPS) VEGETABLE STOCK

150G (4½ OUNCES) GREEN BEANS, TRIMMED, CUT
   INTO 2CM (¾-INCH) LENGTHS ON THE DIAGONAL

2 MEDIUM ZUCCHINI (240G), HALVED LENGTHWAYS,
   SLICED THINLY

400G (12½ OUNCES) CANNED CANNELLINI BEANS,
   DRAINED, RINSED

PESTO

2 CUPS LOOSELY PACKED FRESH BASIL LEAVES

⅓ CUP (25G) FINELY GRATED PARMESAN

¼ CUP (40G) PINE NUTS, TOASTED

½ CLOVE GARLIC, PEELED

½ CUP (125ML) EXTRA VIRGIN OLIVE OIL

1 Heat oil in a large saucepan over medium heat. Cook sage, garlic and leek, stirring, for 3 minutes or until leek is soft. Add parsnip, celery and kale; cook, stirring, for 2 minutes or until kale is bright green. Add stock, bring to the boil; reduce heat to low. Simmer for 15 minutes or until parsnip is almost tender.

2 Add green beans, zucchini and cannellini beans; cook for 5 minutes or until zucchini is just tender. Season to taste.

3 Meanwhile, make pesto.

4 Ladle soup into bowls. Serve topped with pesto.

PESTO Blend or process ingredients until smooth. Transfer to a small bowl; season to taste.

spaghettini niçoise

SERVES 4

This riff on the classic French favourite, niçoise salad, is equally enjoyable served warm or at room temperature. Easy to prepare in advance, it's a great addition to your repertoire of workday lunches and makes excellent picnic fare. Omit the chilli if you prefer.

TIP You can grill tuna steaks for 1 minute each side on a heated oiled grill pan (or barbecue) instead of using canned tuna, if you like.

PREP + COOK TIME 30 MINUTES

250G (8 OUNCES) SPAGHETTINI

4 EGGS

425G (13½ OUNCES) CANNED TUNA CHUNKS IN OLIVE OIL, DRAINED, FLAKED (SEE TIP)

⅓ CUP (55G) PITTED KALAMATA OLIVES, CHOPPED COARSELY

250G (8 OUNCES) CHERRY TOMATOES, HALVED

⅓ CUP (50G) PINE NUTS, TOASTED

100G (3 OUNCES) BABY ROCKET (ARUGULA) LEAVES

½ TEASPOON DRIED CHILLI FLAKES

LEMON MUSTARD DRESSING

2 TABLESPOONS EXTRA VIRGIN OLIVE OIL

1 TABLESPOON FINELY GRATED LEMON RIND

¼ CUP (60ML) LEMON JUICE

1 CLOVE GARLIC, CRUSHED

1 TABLESPOON DIJON MUSTARD

1 TABLESPOON BABY CAPERS

1 Make lemon mustard dressing.

2 Cook pasta in a large saucepan of boiling salted water until almost tender; drain. Return to pan.

3 Meanwhile, place eggs in a small saucepan, cover with cold water; bring to the boil. Cook for 2 minutes or until soft-boiled; drain. Rinse under cold water; drain. When cool enough to handle, peel eggs.

4 Add tuna, olives, tomatoes, pine nuts, rocket and dressing to pasta in pan; toss gently. Season to taste.

5 Serve pasta topped with halved soft-boiled eggs and chilli flakes.

LEMON MUSTARD DRESSING Place ingredients in a screw-top jar; shake well. Season to taste. (Makes ½ cup)

barbecued calamari fattoush salad
SERVES 4

Orginally created as a way of using day-old pitta, a fattoush salad gives new life to stale bread by frying it until crisp and combining it with fresh vegetables for texture and taste. Calamari, a mollusc, is eaten all across the Mediterranean region. Grilled, deep fried or stuffed, together with its ink, it gives flavour and colour to Spanish and Italian dishes such as paella, risotto, soups and pasta.

TIPS For details on how to clean calamari, see Glossary, page 235. You could use cleaned squid hoods instead. If you are having difficulty splitting the pitta breads open, microwave on HIGH (100%) for 10 seconds. The steam from heating in the microwave usually makes it easier to open the bread.

PREP + COOK TIME 50 MINUTES (+ REFRIGERATION)

1½ TEASPOONS CUMIN SEEDS

1 TEASPOON GROUND CORIANDER

2 CLOVES GARLIC, CRUSHED

½ TEASPOON DRIED CHILLI FLAKES

¼ CUP (60ML) EXTRA VIRGIN OLIVE OIL

2 TABLESPOONS LEMON JUICE

6 MEDIUM CALAMARI (720G), CLEANED (SEE TIPS)

3 MEDIUM TOMATOES (450G), CHOPPED COARSELY

1½ TEASPOONS SEA SALT FLAKES

1 LEBANESE CUCUMBER (130G), HALVED
   LENGTHWAYS, SEEDED, SLICED THINLY

1 CUP FRESH MINT LEAVES

1 CUP FRESH FLAT-LEAF PARSLEY LEAVES

2 SMALL WHOLEMEAL POCKET PITTA BREADS (160G),
   SPLIT IN HALF (SEE TIPS)

1 Heat a small frying pan over medium heat. Cook cumin seeds and coriander, stirring, for 2 minutes or until toasted and fragrant. Transfer to a medium bowl, add garlic, chilli, oil and juice; stir to combine. Reserve 2 tablespoons of the spice mixture in a small bowl.

2 Using a sharp knife, cut the calamari hoods in half lengthways. Score inside surface of calamari in a criss-cross pattern at 1cm (½-inch) intervals. Cut into 4cm (1½-inch) strips. Add calamari hoods and tentacles to spice mixture in bowl; toss to coat. Refrigerate calamari for 2 hours.

3 Meanwhile, combine tomato and salt in a colander; stand in the sink for 10 minutes to drain. Place tomato, cucumber, mint and parsley in a medium bowl; toss to combine.

4 Cook pitta and calamari hoods and tentacles on a heated oiled grill plate (or pan or barbecue) until pitta are toasted and calamari is just cooked through.

5 Break pitta into bite-sized pieces. Add reserved spice mixture and half the pitta to tomato mixture; toss to combine. Serve calamari with salad and remaining pitta.

chicken skewers with peach caprese salad

SERVES 4

Caprese salad should be simplicity itself, comprised of layers of sliced fresh mozzarella, basil and luscious sun-ripened tomatoes, seasoned only with salt and olive oil. Traditionally served as an antipasto (starter), here we have made our caprese a little more substantial with the addition of grilled chicken skewers and peach cheeks, which complement the richness of the buffalo mozzarella.

TIPS You can use chilli-infused olive oil for marinating the chicken, if you like. Buffalo mozzarella has a tangier flavour than cow's milk mozzarella, which may be used instead. Swap heirloom tomatoes for regular cherry tomatoes, if preferred. If using bamboo skewers, soak them for 10 minutes in boiling water before using to prevent them burning during cooking.

PREP + COOK TIME 25 MINUTES

400G (12½ OUNCES) CHICKEN BREAST FILLETS, CUT INTO 2CM (1-INCH) PIECES

1½ TABLESPOONS EXTRA VIRGIN OLIVE OIL (SEE TIPS)

4 MEDIUM PEACHES (600G), CHEEKS REMOVED

250G (8 OUNCES) BUFFALO MOZZARELLA, TORN

2 MEDIUM TOMATOES (300G), SLICED

400G (12½ OUNCES) MIXED HEIRLOOM CHERRY TOMATOES, HALVED, QUATERED IF LARGE

½ CUP FRESH SMALL BASIL LEAVES

1 TABLESPOON WHITE WINE VINEGAR

PISTACHIO MINT PESTO

½ CUP (70G) PISTACHIOS

1½ CUPS FRESH MINT LEAVES

1 CUP FRESH FLAT-LEAF PARSLEY LEAVES

1 CLOVE GARLIC, CRUSHED

2 TEASPOONS FINELY GRATED LEMON RIND

2 TEASPOONS LEMON JUICE

½ CUP (125ML) EXTRA VIRGIN OLIVE OIL

1 Make pistachio mint pesto.

2 Combine chicken and 1 tablespoon of the oil in a medium bowl; season. Thread onto four skewers.

3 Cook chicken on a heated oiled grill plate (or pan or barbecue) for 8 minutes. Add peaches to grill plate; cook for a further 2 minutes or until chicken is cooked through and peaches are golden.

4 Layer grilled peaches with mozzarella, tomatoes and basil; drizzle with vinegar and remaining oil. Serve salad topped with chicken and pesto.

PISTACHIO MINT PESTO Blend or process ingredients until smooth; season to taste.

prawn, pea & broad bean frittata
SERVES 4

Derived from the Italian word 'friggere' which roughly translated to 'fried', a frittata is an amazingly versatile dish, the perfect vehicle for using up old vegetables and leftover proteins, while relatively simple to cook. It also makes the best packed lunch for work or school, as it can be eaten heated or cool. Serve accompanied with a simple green salad for a complete meal.

TIP If you don't have an ovenproof frying pan, wrap the handle of your pan in several layers of foil.

PREP + COOK TIME 1 HOUR

½ CUP FRESH FLAT-LEAF PARSLEY LEAVES

⅓ CUP FRESH DILL

6 EGGS

½ CUP (125ML) BUTTERMILK

2 TABLESPOONS PACKAGED DRY BREADCRUMBS

1½ CUPS (225G) FROZEN BROAD (FAVA) BEANS

2 TABLESPOONS EXTRA VIRGIN OLIVE OIL

2 MEDIUM ZUCCHINI (240G), HALVED LENGTHWAYS, SLICED THINLY

3 GREEN ONIONS (SCALLIONS), SLICED THINLY

2 CLOVES GARLIC, CRUSHED

2 CUPS (240G) FROZEN PEAS, THAWED

500G (1 POUND) COOKED MEDIUM KING PRAWNS (SHRIMP), SHELLED, DEVEINED

⅓ CUP (80G) FIRM RICOTTA

LEMON HALVES, TO SERVE

1 Coarsely chop half the herbs; reserve remaining herbs. Whisk chopped herbs, eggs, buttermilk and breadcrumbs in a large bowl; season.

2 Cook broad beans in a large saucepan of boiling water for 2 minutes or until just tender; drain. Refresh under cold running water, drain well. Remove grey skins.

3 Preheat oven to 180°C/350°F.

4 Heat oil in a 21cm (8½-inch) ovenproof frying pan over medium heat; cook zucchini and green onion, stirring, for 5 minutes or until soft. Add garlic, peas and broad beans; cook, stirring, for 1 minute or until fragrant. Add egg mixture, gently shake pan to distribute mixture; reduce heat to low-medium. Cook, without stirring, for 5 minutes or until edge is set. Top with prawns and crumbled ricotta.

5 Bake frittata for 20 minutes or until the centre is just firm.

6 Serve frittata with remaining herbs and the lemon halves.

cavolo nero fritters with pickled beetroot

SERVES 4

Meaning 'black cabbage' in Italian, cavolo nero is championed in many Italian dishes, especially that of the region of Tuscany. The traditional ingredient of minestrone and ribollita, cavolo nero is more delicate and sweet than its relative curly kale, while possessing many of the same nutritional benefits; it is rich in protein, fibre, antioxidants, vitamins A, C, and K, and folate.

TIPS You can use a mandoline or V-slicer to slice the beetroot very thinly. Cooked fritters can be frozen; reheat for a quick breakfast option.

PREP + COOK TIME 35 MINUTES (+ STANDING)

3 LARGE ZUCCHINI (450G), GRATED COARSELY

1 TEASPOON FINE SEA SALT

3 CAVOLO NERO (TUSCAN CABBAGE) LEAVES (30G), TRIMMED, SHREDDED FINELY

2 TABLESPOONS CHOPPED FRESH MINT LEAVES

¼ CUP (40G) WHOLEMEAL PLAIN (ALL-PURPOSE) FLOUR

2 CLOVES GARLIC, CRUSHED

2 EGGS, BEATEN LIGHTLY

⅓ CUP (80ML) EXTRA VIRGIN OLIVE OIL

1 TABLESPOON APPLE CIDER VINEGAR

½ TEASPOON HONEY

100G (3 OUNCES) GREEK FETTA, CRUMBLED

2 TABLESPOONS SUNFLOWER SEED KERNELS, TOASTED

FRESH MINT LEAVES, TO SERVE

PICKLED BEETROOT

3 SMALL BEETROOT (BEETS) (300G), PEELED, SLICED THINLY (SEE TIPS)

2 TABLESPOONS APPLE CIDER VINEGAR

1 Combine zucchini and salt in a colander; stand in the sink for 10 minutes to drain. Using your hands, squeeze excess liquid from zucchini. Place zucchini, cavolo nero, mint, flour, garlic and egg in a medium bowl; season. Mix well to combine.

2 Meanwhile, make pickled beetroot.

3 Heat half the oil in a large non-stick frying pan over medium heat. Add ¼-cup measures of mixture to pan, flatten slightly; cook for 5 minutes on each side or until golden and crisp. Drain on paper towel; cover to keep warm. Repeat with remaining mixture to make eight fritters.

4 Whisk remaining oil, vinegar, honey and reserved pickling liquid in a small bowl until combined.

5 Place fritters on a platter, top with beetroot and fetta. Before serving, drizzle with dressing and sprinkle with sunflower seeds and mint.

PICKLED BEETROOT Combine beetroot and vinegar in a bowl; season. Stand for 5 minutes. Drain; reserve pickling liquid for honey dressing.

sardine & golden tomato bruschetta
SERVES 4

Sardines have been long relegated to 'poor man's' food, but this little fish is a powerhouse of nutrition: a small serving of sardines once a day can provide 13% of vitamin B2; roughly one-quarter of niacin; and about 150% of the recommended daily value of vitamin B12. It's also a great source of omega-3, which has an array of health benefits related to its anti-inflammatory properties.

TIPS You can ask the fishmonger to clean and fillet the sardines for you. Use yellow grape tomatoes instead of cherry tomatoes, if you like.

PREP + COOK TIME 30 MINUTES (+ REFRIGERATION)

1 TEASPOON FENNEL SEEDS, CRUSHED LIGHTLY

2 TEASPOONS SEA SALT FLAKES

2 CLOVES GARLIC, CHOPPED FINELY

500G (1 POUND) FRESH SARDINES, CLEANED,
FILLETED, WITH TAILS INTACT (SEE TIPS)

1KG (2 POUNDS) YELLOW CHERRY TOMATOES
(SEE TIPS)

¼ CUP (60ML) EXTRA VIRGIN OLIVE OIL

1 LOAF CIABATTA BREAD (450G), SLICED, TOASTED

SMALL FRESH BASIL LEAVES AND LEMON WEDGES,
TO SERVE

BASIL & CAPERBERRY OIL

1 CUP FIRMLY-PACKED FRESH BASIL LEAVES

½ CUP (125ML) EXTRA VIRGIN OLIVE OIL

¼ CUP (40G) CAPERBERRIES

2 TEASPOONS FINELY GRATED LEMON RIND

2 TABLESPOONS LEMON JUICE

1 Make basil and caperberry oil.

2 Combine fennel seeds, salt and garlic in a small bowl; season. Rub fennel mixture over sardine fillets. Cover; refrigerate for 30 minutes.

3 Preheat grill (broiler). Toss tomatoes in half the oil on an oven tray. Place under grill for 10 minutes or until tomatoes are just starting to blister. Cool slightly.

4 Place tomatoes and basil and caperberry oil in a large bowl; toss gently to combine. Season to taste.

5 Heat remaining oil in a large frying pan or grill plate; cook sardines, in batches, for 2 minutes on each side or until cooked.

6 Place sardines on toasted bread; spoon tomato mixture on top, pressing gently to allow tomato juices to soak into the bread. Top with basil leaves; serve with lemon wedges.

BASIL & CAPERBERRY OIL Blend or process ingredients until smooth; season to taste.

Portable
Lunches

roasted carrot, radish & egg salad with romesco sauce

SERVES 4

Originating in the Catalonia area of Spain, romesco is a sauce consisting of blended almonds and red capsicum. During the springtime, romesco is served as a dip for calçots, a spring onion native to Catalonia, which are roasted over an open fire until charred. The charred layer is then removed and the tender part dipped into the romesco. It is a great dairy-free alternative to creamy sauces and pesto.

TIP Traditionally used to accompany fish, you could also pair the romesco sauce with lamb or chicken, or serve with crudités and crisp breads as a tasty dip.

PREP + COOK TIME 40 MINUTES

800G (1½ POUNDS) RAINBOW BABY (DUTCH) CARROTS, TRIMMED

1½ TABLESPOONS EXTRA VIRGIN OLIVE OIL

4 EGGS

300G (9½ OUNCE) SMALL RADISHES, TRIMMED, HALVED

⅓ CUP FRESH FLAT-LEAF PARSLEY LEAVES

ROMESCO SAUCE

260G (8½-OUNCE) JAR ROASTED RED CAPSICUMS (BELL PEPPERS), DRAINED

1 CLOVE GARLIC, CRUSHED

½ CUP (80G) BLANCHED ALMONDS, ROASTED

2 TABLESPOONS SHERRY VINEGAR

1 TEASPOON SMOKED PAPRIKA

2 TABLESPOONS CHOPPED FRESH FLAT-LEAF PARSLEY LEAVES

⅓ CUP (80ML) EXTRA VIRGIN OLIVE OIL

1 Preheat oven to 200°C/400°F.

2 Place carrots on a large oven tray, drizzle with oil; season with salt. Roast for 20 minutes or until tender and lightly browned.

3 Meanwhile, make romesco sauce.

4 Place eggs in a small saucepan, cover with cold water; bring to the boil. Cook for 2 minutes or until soft-boiled; drain. Rinse under cold water; drain. When cool enough to handle, peel eggs; tear in half.

5 Place carrots, radish and eggs on a platter. Top with parsley; season with pepper. Serve with romesco sauce.

ROMESCO SAUCE Process ingredients until smooth; season to taste.

hearty italian lentil & vegetable soup

SERVES 4

While meaty stews are often the comfort food of choice when the weather gets chilly, a big bowl of lentil soup is a great vegetarian substitute. Lentils have the second-highest ratio of protein per kilojoules of any legume, after soybeans, and are rich in folate, vitamin B6 and iron.

TIP To make this soup vegetarian, use vegetable stock instead of chicken stock and use a vegetarian parmesan.

PREP + COOK TIME 50 MINUTES

1 TABLESPOON EXTRA VIRGIN OLIVE OIL

1 MEDIUM ONION (150G), CHOPPED FINELY

3 CLOVES GARLIC, CRUSHED

2 TEASPOONS FINELY GRATED FRESH GINGER

1 TEASPOON CUMIN SEEDS, CRUSHED LIGHTLY

1 FRESH LONG RED CHILLI, CHOPPED FINELY

1 MEDIUM CARROT (120G), CHOPPED FINELY

2 TRIMMED CELERY STALKS (200G),
   CHOPPED FINELY

2 FRESH BAY LEAVES

3 FRESH THYME SPRIGS, PLUS EXTRA TO SERVE

1¼ CUPS (185G) DRIED FRENCH-STYLE
   GREEN LENTILS, RINSED

¼ CUP (70G) TOMATO PASTE

1.5 LITRES (6 CUPS) CHICKEN STOCK

1½ TABLESPOONS LEMON JUICE

⅓ CUP (25G) FINELY GRATED PARMESAN

1 FRESH LONG RED CHILLI, EXTRA, SLICED THINLY

1 Heat oil in a large saucepan over medium-high heat; cook onion, garlic, ginger, cumin, long chilli, carrot and celery, stirring, for 10 minutes or until vegetables are softened.

2 Add bay leaves, thyme, lentils, tomato paste and stock, bring to the boil; reduce heat to low. Cook for 20 minutes or until lentils are tender. Stir in juice; season to taste.

3 Ladle soup into bowls, top with parmesan and extra chilli. Sprinkle with extra thyme before serving, if you like.

roast tomato soup with broccoli pesto

SERVES 4

Tomatoes feature heavily in Mediterranean dishes, both in their raw state and cooked. While tomatoes are both nutritious and extremely tasty picked straight from the vine, cooking tomatoes actually increases the level of lycopene present in the vegetable, a phytochemical which has significant antioxidant properties, while also being responsible for their bright red colour.

TIPS To make this vegetarian, use vegetable stock instead of chicken stock and use a vegetarian parmesan in the pesto. Soup and broccoli pesto are suitable to freeze, separately, for up to 3 months.

PREP + COOK TIME 1 HOUR (+ STANDING)

1KG (2 POUNDS) VINE-RIPENED TOMATOES, QUARTERED

3 CLOVES GARLIC, UNPEELED

3 SPRIGS FRESH THYME

1 MEDIUM ONION (150G), CHOPPED

⅓ CUP (80ML) EXTRA VIRGIN OLIVE OIL

3 CUPS (750ML) CHICKEN STOCK

1 TABLESPOON PINE NUTS, TOASTED

SMALL FRESH BASIL LEAVES, TO SERVE

BROCCOLI PESTO

100G (3 OUNCES) BROCCOLI, CHOPPED

1 CLOVE GARLIC, CRUSHED

1½ TABLESPOONS PINE NUTS, TOASTED

1½ TABLESPOONS FINELY GRATED PARMESAN

1½ TABLESPOONS COARSELY CHOPPED FRESH BASIL LEAVES

¼ CUP (60ML) EXTRA VIRGIN OLIVE OIL

1 Preheat oven to 220°C/425°F.

2 Place tomatoes, garlic, thyme and onion in a roasting pan; season. Drizzle with ¼ cup of the oil; toss to coat tomatoes. Roast for 30 minutes or until tomatoes are very soft and browned around the edges.

3 Meanwhile, make broccoli pesto.

4 Transfer roasted tomatoes and onion to a medium saucepan. Remove thyme stalks. Squeeze garlic out of skins; add to tomato mixture. Add stock to pan and bring to the boil. Cool for 10 minutes. Blend or process mixture until smooth; return soup to pan. Stir over low heat until hot; season to taste.

5 Ladle soup into bowls; top with broccoli pesto, pine nuts and basil. Drizzle with remaining oil.

BROCCOLI PESTO Cook broccoli in a small saucepan of boiling water for 2 minutes; drain. Refresh under cold running water; drain well. Process broccoli, garlic, pine nuts, parmesan and basil until finely chopped. With motor operating, gradually pour in oil; process until combined. Season to taste.

chicken, zucchini & freekeh soup

SERVES 4

Freekeh is made from roasted young green wheat. Nutritionally freekeh stacks up impressively; it has a low GI, four times the fibre of brown rice and is higher in protein than regular wheat. The name freekeh comes from the word 'farik' which refers to the way that freekeh is threshed, or 'rubbed', to remove its tough and inedible outer bran layer.

TIPS Freekeh is a wheat product so it does contain gluten; it is available from health food stores, some delicatessens and greengrocers. For a more intense flavour, use homemade chicken stock instead of water.

PREP + COOK TIME 45 MINUTES

½ CUP (100G) CRACKED GREEN-WHEAT FREEKEH (SEE TIPS)

1 TABLESPOON EXTRA VIRGIN OLIVE OIL

1 MEDIUM LEEK (350G), WHITE PART ONLY, HALVED, SLICED THINLY

4 CLOVES GARLIC, SLICED THINLY

1.25 LITRES (5 CUPS) WATER (SEE TIPS)

4 CHICKEN THIGH FILLETS (680G)

150G (4½ OUNCES) GREEN BEANS, TRIMMED, CUT INTO 2CM (¾-INCH) LENGTHS

1 LARGE ZUCCHINI (150G), HALVED LENGTHWAYS, SLICED THINLY

½ CUP (60G) FROZEN PEAS

1 TEASPOON FINELY GRATED LEMON RIND

2 TABLESPOONS LEMON JUICE

2 TABLESPOONS CHOPPED FRESH FLAT-LEAF PARSLEY LEAVES

1 Place freekeh in a medium saucepan, cover with water; bring to the boil. Reduce heat to low; cook, partially covered, for 15 minutes or until almost tender. Drain.

2 Meanwhile, heat oil a large saucepan over medium heat; cook leek, stirring, for 4 minutes or until softened. Add garlic; cook, stirring, for 2 minutes.

3 Add the water and chicken, bring to the boil; reduce heat to low. Cook, covered, for 12 minutes or until chicken is cooked. Remove chicken from stock; shred meat. Return shredded chicken to pan with green beans and freekeh, season to taste; cook for 5 minutes. Add zucchini and peas; cook for 3 minutes or until tender. Stir in rind and juice.

4 Ladle soup into bowls; top with parsley. Season to taste.

salad niçoise

SERVES 4

Referred to as "one of the best combinations of salad ingredients ever invented", the salad niçoise is named after its place of origin, the French city of Nice. Popularised by celebrity chefs, salad niçoise is now found all over the world, and like all great dishes, is the centre of great debate as to what should or should not go into it, and whether or not you should even include cooked vegetables at all.

TIPS Swap canned tuna in oil for fresh tuna, if you like. Omit the caperberries, if you prefer.

PREP + COOK TIME 45 MINUTES

600G (1¼ POUNDS) BABY NEW POTATOES, HALVED

200G (6½ OUNCES) GREEN BEANS, TRIMMED, HALVED

3 EGGS

2 X 200G (6½-OUNCE) THICK-CUT TUNA STEAKS (SEE TIPS)

1 TABLESPOON EXTRA VIRGIN OLIVE OIL

⅓ SMALL RED ONION (50G), SLICED THINLY

250G (8 OUNCES) CHERRY TOMATOES, HALVED

⅓ CUP (40G) PITTED SMALL BLACK OLIVES

⅓ CUP (55G) CAPERBERRIES, RINSED (SEE TIPS)

¼ CUP SMALL FRESH BASIL LEAVES

2 TABLESPOONS COARSELY CHOPPED FRESH FLAT-LEAF PARSLEY LEAVES

DRESSING

2 TABLESPOONS EXTRA VIRGIN OLIVE OIL

2 TABLESPOONS WHITE WINE VINEGAR

2 TEASPOONS LEMON JUICE

1 Place potatoes in a small saucepan, cover with cold water; bring to the boil. Cook for 15 minutes or until tender; drain.

2 Meanwhile, boil, steam or microwave beans until tender; drain. Refresh under cold running water; drain well.

3 Make dressing.

4 Place hot potatoes in a large bowl with one-third of the dressing; toss gently to combine.

5 Place eggs in a small saucepan, cover with cold water; bring to the boil. Cook for 2 minutes or until soft-boiled; drain. Rinse under cold water; drain. When eggs are cool enough to handle, peel; tear in half.

6 Brush tuna with oil; season. Heat a large heavy-based frying pan over high heat; cook tuna for 1 minute on each side for medium-rare or until cooked as desired. Cut into thin slices.

7 Add beans, onion, tomatoes, eggs, olives, caperberries, herbs and remaining dressing to bowl; toss gently to combine. Serve topped with tuna.

DRESSING Place ingredients in a small screw-top jar; shake well. Season to taste.

spinach & yoghurt flatbreads with greek bean salad

SERVES 4

Most people in the Mediterranean region could not imagine a day going by without the consumption of bread in one form or another. Fresh bread is surely one of the world's greatest comforts, and these simple flatbreads are a hassle-free way of preparing your own. Make the dough ahead of time and cook it to order to accompany a light lunch or dinner, or to have as a light meal on its own.

TIPS Keep flatbread warm in a preheated 120°C/250°F oven. Use purchased tzatziki instead of making your own, if preferred.

DO-AHEAD Make spinach dough a day ahead, cover and refrigerate until needed. Bring to room temperature before rolling out.

PREP + COOK TIME 45 MINUTES (+ STANDING)

250G (8 OUNCES) FROZEN CHOPPED SPINACH, THAWED

1 CUP (150G) SELF-RAISING FLOUR

½ CUP (140G) GREEK-STYLE YOGHURT

1 CLOVE GARLIC, CRUSHED

2 TABLESPOONS EXTRA VIRGIN OLIVE OIL

200G (6½ OUNCES) TZATZIKI (SEE PAGE 158)

LEMON WEDGES, TO SERVE

GREEK BEAN SALAD

125G (4 OUNCES) MIXED CHERRY TOMATOES, HALVED

1 LEBANESE CUCUMBER (130G), QUARTERED LENGTHWAYS, SLICED

½ CUP (100G) CANNED CANNELLINI BEANS, DRAINED, RINSED

¼ CUP (30G) PITTED BLACK OLIVES, HALVED

¼ CUP LOOSELY PACKED FRESH OREGANO LEAVES

100G (3 OUNCES) GREEK FETTA, CRUMBLED

1 Place spinach in a clean tea towel. Squeeze over a sink to remove as much excess liquid as possible. Place spinach, flour, yoghurt and garlic in a large bowl; season. Use your hands to bring ingredients together and form a rough dough. Cover; stand dough for 1 hour.

2 Make greek bean salad.

3 Divide dough into eight balls. Roll out each ball of dough on a floured surface until 2mm (⅛-inch) thick.

4 Heat 1 teaspoon of the oil in a large heavy-based frying pan over medium heat; cook one flatbread for 1 minute on each side or until golden. Remove from pan; cover to keep warm (see tips). Repeat with remaining oil and dough.

5 Top flatbreads evenly with tzatziki and salad; serve with lemon wedges.

GREEK BEAN SALAD Place ingredients in a large bowl; toss gently to combine. Season to taste.

The Italian diet

Italy was unified as a single nation in the 1860s but before then it comprised small, independent states each with, literally, their own distinctive flavour. A long finger of a country surrounded by the Adriatic Sea on one side and the Mediterranean on the other, food traditions are influenced by fishing and farming. Clear regional differences still abound and nowhere is this more evident than in the cuisine. In parts of the north, fresh pasta and dairy foods hold sway; cooks are more likely to use butter than olive oil and dishes can be opulent. In other areas there's more frugality; Tuscany's bread and tomato soups reflect this. However, no matter where you look in Italy, vegetables, dried beans and legumes, cereals like rice, farro and polenta and, around coastal stretches, fish such as snapper, are key to the traditional diet. Minestrone, and other bean and vegetable-rich soups, vegetable-based antipasti and vegetable-sauce rice and pasta are eaten regularly, and never viewed as meat-free penance.

The south is influenced by a dry, hot climate and proximity to the Mediterranean Sea, with olive oil and a variety of crops such as olives, citrus fruits, figs, tomatoes, grapes, eggplants, wheat and almonds, at the heart of the cuisine. Goat, sheep and buffalo milk cheeses abound and red wine is regularly enjoyed. This combination is core to the Mediterranean diet, but here, they have their own unique spin. Particularly on the islands of Sicily and Sardinia, where certain ethnic staples (such as sesame seeds, couscous and wild mint) speak of a distinctive set of exotic influences, mainly Arab, Greek and Spanish.

Researchers have been particularly interested in the residents of mountain villages in the western part of Sicily, as the number of centenarians there is incredibly high. Their diet has a particularly low glycemic index, which translates to loads of vegetables eaten daily, a little dairy, not much meat or pasta, very rare snacks, virtually no sweets and no modern preserved foods. Lifestyle habits such as daily walking, shopping locally, living in tight-knit family groups and eating together are also held as key indicators for longevity and overall good health. While not all of Sicily lives and eats exactly like this pocket in the Sicani mountains, the cuisine in general reflects the dependence on vegetables and lean protein. Classic main course dishes include caponata (a sweet and sour 'relish' based on tomato, zucchini, onion and eggplant) and involtini di melanzane (baked eggplant rolls). Seafood (tuna, sardines, squid, swordfish, prawns, clams and the like) is the core protein, supplemented by sheep's milk cheeses such as pecorino and ricotta.

Sardinia is another special island whose diet and lifestyle have caught the attention of scientists; people here live, on average, to a ripe old age. While the rugged terrain has kept outsiders away and the gene pool pure, it's the diet, high in vegetable-derived nutrients, olive oil, lemon, wild herbs and garlic, that's the key pointer. It's also believed that Sardinian cheeses, much of them made using raw goat's milk and full of gut-boosting microbes, play an important part too. Chickpeas, dried broad beans, tomatoes, fennel and island-grown almonds feature, as does milk thistle tea, brewed from a local plant and full of antioxidant and anti-inflammatory benefits.

THE ITALIAN LIFESTYLE

OLIVE OIL
Used liberally in Italian food, olive oil contributes to the low consumption of saturated fats.

SEASONAL GREENS
The basis of main courses, including elaborate pasta sauces. Italy's warm climate means growing seasons are very long and vegetables plentiful.

VEGETABLES
Eggplant, tomatoes, cauliflower, zucchini, fennel, onions, capsicum and broccoli rabe are all used abudantly.

PASTA
Made from nutritious triticum wheat or semolina durum flours; fresh egg dough pasta is commonly used in the north, while dried pastas are widely eaten across the region.

SEAFOOD
Dishes originating in coastal areas often champion seafood. Inland, shepherding is a traditional occupation so goat, lamb and raw cheeses made from their milk, are also abundant.

GRAINS, BEANS & PULSES
Rice, chickpeas, lentils, polenta, dried broad beans, farro, barley, and oats are among the regional grains, beans and pulses used.

cauliflower pastilla triangles

MAKES 9

Pastilla is a traditional Moroccan pie served on special occasions. Traditionally filled with a lightly spiced mix of poultry and nuts, here we've made a vegetarian version starring cauliflower. Saffron is one of the most expensive spices in the world by weight, this is because it consists of the dried stigmas of the crocus plant; a kilogram of saffron requires 110,000–170,000 flowers.

SERVING SUGGESTION
Serve with Greek-style yoghurt, if you like.

PREP + COOK TIME 1 HOUR 20 MINUTES (+ STANDING)

PINCH SAFFRON THREADS

1 TABLESPOON HOT WATER

2 TABLESPOONS EXTRA VIRGIN OLIVE OIL

2 MEDIUM RED ONIONS (340G), CHOPPED FINELY

2 CLOVES GARLIC, CRUSHED

1 TEASPOON GROUND TURMERIC

1 TEASPOON GROUND GINGER

¾ TEASPOON GROUND CINNAMON

½ SMALL CAULIFLOWER (500G), CHOPPED FINELY

1 CUP (160G) ROASTED BLANCHED ALMONDS, CHOPPED COARSELY

1 CUP COARSELY CHOPPED FRESH CORIANDER (CILANTRO) LEAVES

1 CUP COARSELY CHOPPED FRESH FLAT-LEAF PARSLEY LEAVES

9 SHEETS FILLO PASTRY

½ CUP (125ML) EXTRA VIRGIN OLIVE OIL, EXTRA

LEMON WEDGES, TO SERVE

1 Combine saffron and the water in a small bowl.

2 Heat oil in a large frying pan over medium heat; cook onion, garlic, turmeric, ginger and ½ teaspoon of the ground cinnamon for 5 minutes or until onion softens. Add cauliflower; cook, stirring, for 10 minutes or until tender. Season with salt. Add saffron mixture; cook for 1 minute or until water evaporates. Transfer to a large bowl; stir in almonds and herbs. Leave to cool completely.

3 Preheat oven to 180°C/350°F. Oil an oven tray.

4 Brush one sheet of pastry with a little of the extra oil; cut in half lengthways, place one strip on the other. Keep remaining sheets covered with baking paper topped with a clean, damp tea towel to prevent them from drying out. Place ⅓ cup cauliflower mixture in a corner of the pastry strip, leaving a 1cm (½-inch) border. Fold opposite corner of pastry diagonally across filling to form a triangle; continue folding to end of pastry sheet, retaining triangular shape. Place triangle, seam-side down, on tray. Repeat with remaining pastry, oil and cauliflower filling.

5 Brush triangles with a little more oil; dust with remaining cinnamon. Bake for 30 minutes or until pastry is browned lightly.

6 Serve warm with lemon wedges.

chilli sardine pasta with pine nuts & currants

SERVES 4

Dried fruits have long been a important component of the Mediterranean diet, eaten on their own, or as the sweet element in traditional desserts. True currants are from the region of Corinth, and are small and black with a intense sweet flavour. Greece is still the primary producer of currants, with about 80% of total world production coming from the country,

TIPS Sardines in flavoured oils are available from major supermarkets and delicatessens. Use a mandoline or V-slicer to slice the fennel very thinly.

PREP + COOK TIME 20 MINUTES

400G (12½ OUNCES) SPAGHETTI

¼ CUP (60ML) EXTRA VIRGIN OLIVE OIL

2 X 110G (3½-OUNCE) CANS SARDINES IN LEMON, CHILLI AND GARLIC OIL (SEE TIPS)

¼ CUP (40G) PINE NUTS, TOASTED

¼ CUP (40G) CURRANTS

2 TABLESPOONS LEMON JUICE

2 TEASPOONS FINELY GRATED LEMON RIND

½ CUP FRESH FLAT-LEAF PARSLEY LEAVES, CHOPPED COARSELY

120G (4 OUNCES) BABY ROCKET (ARUGULA) LEAVES

1 BABY FENNEL BULB (130G), TRIMMED, SLICED THINLY (SEE TIPS)

LEMON WEDGES, TO SERVE

1 Cook pasta in a large saucepan of boiling salted water until almost tender; drain, reserving 1 cup of the cooking water.

2 Meanwhile, heat ¼ cup of the oil in a large frying pan over medium heat. Add sardines; cook, stirring occasionally, for 2 minutes or until heated through.

3 Add pasta, pine nuts, currants and juice to sardines. Heat pan over high heat. Add enough reserved water to moisten pasta; cook, stirring, for 2 minutes. Season to taste.

4 Combine the lemon rind and parsley in a small bowl; stir half through pasta.

5 Place rocket and fennel in a bowl.

6 Divide pasta among four bowls; sprinkle with remaining lemon rind mixture and drizzle with remaining oil. Serve with rocket and fennel salad and lemon wedges.

chicken with zucchini 'noodles', fetta & salsa verde

SERVES 4

While to a true Italian, these zucchini 'noodles' (or zoodles) may seems like heresy, they are a great alternative to pasta when you are looking to avoid the carbs and have a light summer meal. They also help to increase your vegetable consumption, and lower your overall kilojoule intake.

TIP A spiraliser is a kitchen gadget that cuts vegetables into long thin spirals. If you don't have one, you can use a mandoline or V-slicer.

PREP + COOK TIME 35 MINUTES

4 CHICKEN BREAST FILLETS (800G), HALVED HORIZONTALLY

1 TABLESPOON EXTRA VIRGIN OLIVE OIL

5 MEDIUM ZUCCHINI (500G)

⅓ CUP (25G) FLAKED ALMONDS, TOASTED

100G (3 OUNCES) GOAT'S FETTA, CRUMBLED

¼ CUP FRESH FLAT-LEAF PARSLEY LEAVES

SALSA VERDE

½ CUP COARSELY CHOPPED FRESH FLAT-LEAF PARSLEY

¼ CUP COARSELY CHOPPED FRESH BASIL

1 CLOVE GARLIC, CRUSHED

2 TEASPOONS BABY CAPERS

1 TEASPOON DIJON MUSTARD

¼ CUP (60ML) EXTRA VIRGIN OLIVE OIL

2 TEASPOONS RED WINE VINEGAR

1 Season chicken. Heat oil in a large frying pan over medium-high heat; cook chicken, in batches, for 4 minutes on each side or until browned and cooked through. Transfer to a plate; stand, covered loosely with foil.

2 Meanwile, using a vegetable spiraliser (see tip), cut zucchini into noodles.

3 Make salsa verde.

4 Top zucchini with chicken, spoonfuls of salsa verde, almonds, fetta and parsley. Serve with remaining salsa verde.

SALSA VERDE Combine herbs, garlic and capers in a small bowl; whisk in mustard, oil and vinegar until thickened. Season to taste. (Makes ⅔ cup)

roasted cauliflower, cavolo nero & spiced chickpea salad

SERVES 4

Chickpeas are an often overlooked legume, full of protein, fibre and folate. One of the oldest cultivated legumes in the world with 7,500-year-old remains found in the Middle East, proving our taste for the little ingredient has existed for centuries. Chickpeas can be cooked and eaten cold in salads, ground into flour, fried as falafel, baked into a flatbread, used in stews, or blended to make hummus.

TIPS Pomegranate molasses is available from Middle-Eastern food stores, major supermarkets, specialty food shops and some delicatessens. This salad can be served warm or at room temperature.

PREP + COOK TIME 40 MINUTES

1 SMALL CAULIFLOWER (680G), TRIMMED,
  CUT INTO SMALL FLORETS

220G (7 OUNCES) BRUSSELS SPROUTS,
  TRIMMED, SLICED

2 TABLESPOONS EXTRA VIRGIN OLIVE OIL

400G (12½ OUNCES) CANNED CHICKPEAS
  (GARBANZO BEANS), DRAINED, RINSED

1 TEASPOON SMOKED PAPRIKA

1 TEASPOON GROUND CUMIN

1 TEASPOON GROUND CORIANDER

12 CAVOLO NERO (TUSCAN CABBAGE) LEAVES
  (120G), TRIMMED, TORN

1 FRESH LONG RED CHILLI, SEEDED,
  CHOPPED FINELY

TAHINI DRESSING

1 TABLESPOON TAHINI

1 TABLESPOON POMEGRANATE MOLASSES (SEE TIPS)

1 SMALL CLOVE GARLIC, CRUSHED

¼ CUP (60ML) WATER

1 Preheat oven to 200°C/400°F.

2 Place cauliflower and brussels sprouts on an oven tray; drizzle with half the oil. Season; toss to coat in oil. Place chickpeas on another oven tray; sprinkle with paprika, cumin and coriander. Season; drizzle with remaining oil.

3 Roast vegetables and chickpeas for 25 minutes. Add cavolo nero to vegetables; roast for a further 5 minutes or until vegetables are tender and chickpeas are crisp.

4 Meanwhile, make tahini dressing.

5 Drizzle vegetables and chickpeas with dressing and sprinkle with chilli; serve.

TAHINI DRESSING Combine ingredients in a small bowl; season to taste.

THE MEDITERRANEAN DIET PORTABLE LUNCHES

chermoulla tuna, chickpea & broad bean salad

SERVES 2

Chermoulla is a spice marinade which contains the core ingredients of garlic, cumin, coriander, oil, and salt. Traditionally used to flavour fish or seafood, you could make double the recipe and use it to dress other meats and vegetables, adding a fresh element to simple dishes.

TIPS Purchase sashimi-grade tuna for this recipe. Alternatively, swap the tuna for salmon, if you like. To segment a lemon, use a small sharp knife to cut the top and bottom from lemon. Cut off the rind with the white pith, following the curve of the fruit. Holding the lemon over a bowl, cut down both sides of the white membrane to release each segment. If the chermoulla ingredients aren't blending well, add 1 tablespoon water to the mixture.

PREP + COOK TIME 30 MINUTES (+ REFRIGERATION)

300G (9½-OUNCE) PIECE TUNA STEAK (SEE TIPS)

1 CUP (150G) FROZEN BROAD (FAVA) BEANS

150G (4½ OUNCES) GREEN BEANS, TRIMMED, HALVED LENGTHWAYS

400G (12½ OUNCES) CANNED CHICKPEAS (GARBANZO BEANS), DRAINED, RINSED

½ CUP FRESH FLAT-LEAF PARSLEY LEAVES

1 MEDIUM LEMON (140G), SEGMENTED (SEE TIPS)

1 TABLESPOON LEMON JUICE

1 TABLESPOON EXTRA VIRGIN OLIVE OIL

CHERMOULLA

½ SMALL RED ONION (50G), CHOPPED COARSELY

1 CLOVE GARLIC, PEELED

1 CUP FIRMLY PACKED FRESH CORIANDER (CILANTRO) LEAVES, CHOPPED ROUGHLY

1 CUP FIRMLY PACKED FRESH FLAT-LEAF PARSLEY LEAVES, CHOPPED COARSELY

1 TEASPOON GROUND CUMIN

1 TEASPOON SMOKED PAPRIKA

1 TABLESPOON EXTRA VIRGIN OLIVE OIL

1 Make chermoulla. Reserve three-quarters of the chermoulla to serve.

2 Place tuna in a shallow dish with remaining chermoulla; toss to coat. Cover; refrigerate for 30 minutes.

3 Meanwhile, cook broad beans and green beans in a large saucepan of boiling water for 2 minutes or until just tender; drain. Refresh under cold running water; drain well. Separate broad beans; remove grey skins from broad beans.

4 Cook tuna on a heated oiled grill plate or barbecue over medium heat for 2 minutes each side or until slightly charred on the outside but still rare in the centre; cover loosely with foil, stand for 5 minutes. Cut tuna, across the grain, into slices.

5 Combine broad beans, green beans, chickpeas, parsley and lemon segments in a medium bowl with combined juice and oil. Serve tuna and salad topped with reserved chermoulla.

CHERMOULLA Blend or process ingredients until just combined; season to taste.

spicy prawn & white bean panzanella

SERVES 4

Before the advent of the modern supermarket bread, every cuisine around the world had a recipe for using stale bread – panzanella is Italy's answer to this age-old problem. While starting off as a simple peasant dish born of necessity, panzanella has long been a dish favoured for its simplicity that allows the flavours of good-quality ingredients to shine through.

TIPS If you don't have a zester, you can finely grate the lemon rind instead. You can use marinated fetta instead of goat's cheese. If you like, omit the prawns and add a can of flaked drained tuna in olive oil.

PREP + COOK TIME 20 MINUTES

160G (5 OUNCES) WHOLEGRAIN SOURDOUGH BREAD

OLIVE-OIL SPRAY

1 MEDIUM LEMON (140G)

800G (1½ POUNDS) COOKED MEDIUM KING PRAWNS (SHRIMP)

400G (12½ OUNCES) CANNED CANNELLINI BEANS, DRAINED, RINSED

250G (8 OUNCES) MIXED CHERRY TOMATOES, HALVED

2 LEBANESE CUCUMBERS (260G), CHOPPED

1 SMALL RED ONION (100G), SLICED THINLY

½ CUP (60G) PITTED SICILIAN OLIVES, HALVED

1 FRESH LONG RED CHILLI, SLICED THINLY

1 CUP LOOSELY PACKED FRESH BASIL LEAVES

120G (4 OUNCES) SOFT GOAT'S CHEESE, CRUMBLED

¼ CUP (60ML) EXTRA VIRGIN OLIVE OIL

⅓ CUP (80ML) RED WINE VINEGAR

1 CLOVE GARLIC, CRUSHED

1 Preheat oven to 220°C/425°F. Line a large oven tray with baking paper.

2 Tear bread coarsely into bite-sized pieces, place on lined tray; spray with oil. Bake for 5 minutes or until golden and crisp.

3 Remove rind from lemon into long thin strips with a zester (see tips). Shell and devein prawns, leaving tails intact.

4 Place bread, rind, prawns, beans, tomatoes, cucumber, onion, olives, chilli, basil and half the cheese in a large bowl; toss gently to combine.

5 Combine oil, vinegar and garlic in a small bowl; season to taste. Just before serving, spoon dressing over salad; top with remaining cheese.

mountain rice salad with haloumi

SERVES 4

Haloumi is a Cypriot semi-hard, unripened brined cheese, often made from a mixture of goat's and sheep's milk. Its high melting point allows for it to hold its shape while being either fried or grilled. You shouldn't allow haloumi to become cold after it is cooked, as it becomes chewy and not nearly as delectable as when soft and golden straight from the grill.

TIPS Mountain rice blend is a combination of brown rice, black rice and red rice. You can use frozen peas instead of broad beans, if preferred. Sprinkle with dill sprigs before serving, if you like.

PREP + COOK TIME 50 MINUTES

¼ CUP (60ML) RED WINE VINEGAR

1 TABLESPOON DIJON MUSTARD

¼ CUP (60ML) EXTRA VIRGIN OLIVE OIL

¼ CUP (90G) HONEY

1 CUP (200G) MOUNTAIN RICE BLEND (SEE TIPS)

500G (1 POUND) FROZEN BROAD (FAVA) BEANS

1 BABY FENNEL BULB (130G), TRIMMED,
　　SLICED THINLY

100G (3 OUNCES) CHAMPAGNE RADISHES,
　　SLICED THINLY

¼ CUP COARSELY CHOPPED FRESH DILL

250G (8 OUNCES) HALOUMI, CUT INTO
　　1CM (½-INCH) SLICES

1 Place red wine vinegar, mustard, 2 tablespoons oil and 2 tablespoons honey in a screw-top jar; shake well. Season to taste.

2 Cook rice in a large saucepan of boiling water for 20 minutes or until tender; drain. Rinse under cold water; drain well.

3 Cook broad beans in a large saucepan of boiling water for 2 minutes or until just tender; drain. Refresh under cold running water, drain well; remove grey skins.

4 Place rice in a large bowl with half the dressing; mix well. Add broad beans, fennel, radishes and dill; toss gently to combine.

5 Heat remaining oil in a large non-stick frying pan over medium-high heat; cook haloumi for 1 minute on each side or until golden brown. Drizzle with remaining honey.

6 Place rice salad on a large platter; top with haloumi and pan juices. Just before serving, drizzle with remaining dressing.

Spanish-style fish with smoky eggplant

SERVES 4

Red mullet is a fish particularly favoured in Mediterranean cuisine for its delicate flavour and beautiful colour. Eggplant is rich in anthocyanins, flavonoids that reduce blood pressure and lower risk of cardiovascular disease. It also possesses an abundance of nasunin in its bright purple skin – an antioxidant that protects the lipids in brain cell membranes that let nutrients in and waste out.

TIP Swap sand whiting or butterflied sardine fillets for red mullet, if you like.

PREP + COOK TIME 55 MINUTES (+ STANDING)

4 SMALL EGGPLANTS (400G)

1 MEDIUM RED CAPSICUM (BELL PEPPER) (200G)

1 TEASPOON SMOKED PAPRIKA

2 TABLESPOONS EXTRA VIRGIN OLIVE OIL

12 RED MULLET FILLETS (960G), SKIN ON (SEE TIP)

400G (12½ OUNCES) CANNED CANNELLINI BEANS, DRAINED, RINSED

½ CUP (150G) WHOLE-EGG MAYONNAISE

1 CLOVE GARLIC, CRUSHED

1 TABLESPOON LEMON JUICE

¼ CUP FRESH FLAT-LEAF PARSLEY LEAVES

LEMON CHEEKS, TO SERVE

1 Preheat oven to 200°C/400°F. Line an oven tray with baking paper.

2 Cut eggplant in half lengthways; score flesh at 1cm (½-inch) intervals. Quarter capsicum; discard seeds and membranes. Place eggplant and capsicum, skin-side up, on lined tray. Roast for 30 minutes or until capsicum skin blisters and blackens and eggplant is tender. Transfer to a heatproof bowl; cover for 5 minutes. Peel away vegetable skins. Shred eggplant coarsely; slice capsicum thickly. Season to taste.

3 Meanwhile, combine smoked paprika and half the oil in a medium shallow bowl, add fish; turn to coat. Heat a large non-stick frying pan over high heat; cook fish, in two batches, skin-side first, for 1½ minutes each side or until just cooked through. Transfer to a plate; stand, covered loosely with foil.

4 Meanwile, heat remaining oil in same pan over medium heat; cook beans, stirring, until warmed through. Season to taste.

5 Meanwhile, combine mayonnaise, garlic and juice in a small bowl; season to taste.

6 Combine eggplant, capsicum and beans, top with fish and parsley. Serve with aïoli and lemon cheeks.

grilled vegetable & capsicum relish subs

SERVES 4

These vegetarian sandwiches definitely pack a punch in terms of flavours, with the smoky taste of the grill, the umami of the parmesan-rich pesto and the bite of the capsicum relish.

DO-AHEAD
Capsicum relish can be made in advance and stored in an airtight container in the fridge for up to 1 week.

PREP + COOK TIME 50 MINUTES (+ COOLING)

2 SMALL EGGPLANT (460G), CUT INTO
  1CM (½-INCH) SLICES

200G (6½ OUNCES) PATTY PAN SQUASH,
  CUT INTO 1CM (½-INCH) SLICES

200G (6½ OUNCES) BUTTERNUT PUMPKIN,
  PEELED, SLICED THINLY

OLIVE-OIL SPRAY

4 MINI BAGUETTE ROLLS (680G),
  HALVED LENGTHWAYS

⅓ CUP (65G) PESTO (SEE PAGE 41)

⅓ CUP (80G) SOFT RICOTTA

½ CUP ROCKET (ARUGULA) LEAVES

CAPSICUM RELISH

1 TABLESPOON EXTRA VIRGIN OLIVE OIL

1 SMALL ONION (80G), CHOPPED FINELY

1 CLOVE GARLIC, CRUSHED

1 TEASPOON GROUND CUMIN

½ TEASPOON CHILLI POWDER

2 MEDIUM RED CAPSICUMS (BELL PEPPERS) (400G),
  CHOPPED COARSELY

2 MEDIUM YELLOW CAPSICUMS (BELL PEPPERS)
  (400G), CHOPPED COARSELY

2 TABLESPOONS BROWN SUGAR

2 TABLESPOONS RED WINE VINEGAR

1 Make capsicum relish.

2 Meanwhile, spray eggplant, squash and pumpkin with oil; season. Cook vegetables, in batches, on a heated oiled grill plate (or pan or barbecue) over medium-high heat for 3 minutes each side or until browned and tender.

3 Spread each roll with 1 tablespoon pesto and 1 tablespoon ricotta; top evenly with vegetables, relish and rocket.

CAPSICUM RELISH Heat oil in a medium frying pan over medium heat. Add onion, garlic and spices; cook, covered, for 5 minutes. Add capsicum; cook, covered, stirring occasionally, for 20 minutes or until soft. Stir in sugar and vinegar; cook until syrupy. Cool.

spicy pumpkin & cauliflower with rice & yoghurt dressing

SERVES 4

Greek-style yoghurt is a type of yoghurt that has been strained to remove its whey (liquid remaining in the cheese-making process), with a more sour taste and creamier texture than its commercial counterpart. Rich in calcium, good fats and probiotics, which are essential for good gut health, Greek-style yoghurt is a great addition to your diet for your overall health.

TIPS Swap butternut pumpkin for kent pumpkin, if preferred. Sprinkle with micro herbs before serving, if you like.

SERVING SUGGESTION Serve with roast lamb or barbecued lamb leg steaks or, for a vegetarian option, add a 400g can drained, rinsed chickpeas to the rice at step 3.

PREP + COOK TIME 45 MINUTES

750G (1½ POUNDS) KENT PUMPKIN, CUT INTO THIN WEDGES

750G (1½ POUNDS) CAULIFLOWER, CUT INTO FLORETS

2½ TABLESPOONS EXTRA VIRGIN OLIVE OIL

2 TEASPOONS GROUND CORIANDER

2 TEASPOONS GROUND CUMIN

½ TEASPOON GROUND CINNAMON

½ CUP (100G) BROWN RICE

2 LITRES (8 CUPS) WATER

2 TEASPOONS LEMON JUICE

1 TABLESPOON PEPITAS (PUMPKIN SEED KERNELS)

1 TEASPOON FINELY GRATED LEMON RIND

YOGHURT DRESSING

1 CUP (280G) GREEK-STYLE YOGHURT

2 TABLESPOONS COARSELY CHOPPED FRESH CORIANDER (CILANTRO)

1 TEASPOON FINELY GRATED LEMON RIND

1 TABLESPOON LEMON JUICE

1 Preheat oven to 200°C/400°F.

2 Combine pumpkin, cauliflower, 1 tablespoon of the oil and the spices on a large oven tray until vegetables are well coated; spread evenly in a single layer. Season. Roast for 30 minutes or until vegetables are tender.

3 Meanwhile, place rice and the water in a medium saucepan; bring to the boil. Boil for 25 minutes or until rice is tender. Drain well; transfer to a bowl. Add remaining oil and the lemon juice; stir to combine.

4 Make yoghurt dressing.

5 Spoon rice onto a large platter or among four plates; top evenly with roasted vegetables. Spoon over a little of the dressing, sprinkle with pepitas and rind; serve with remaining dressing.

YOGHURT DRESSING Combine ingredients in a medium bowl; season to taste.

lamb salad with spinach pesto dressing
SERVES 4

While we often think first of nuts, seeds and oily fish as the greatest supplies of omega-3 fats, lamb is also a great source of these fatty acids. It is also an excellent source of protein and vital nutrients like iron, zinc, selenium and vitamin B12. Make sure to buy grass-fed lamb, as the diet of the animal will directly influence the nutritional value of the meat itself.

TIPS The oil from the marinated goat's cheese adds extra depth of flavour to this dish. The cheese we used was marinated in a mixture of olive oil, garlic, thyme and chilli. If you've made your own pesto (see pages 29 or 41), use this instead of baby spinach pesto, if you like, or swap with your favourite purchased pesto.

PREP + COOK TIME **35 MINUTES**

600G (1¼ OUNCES) LAMB BACKSTRAPS
(EYE OF LOIN)

1 CLOVE GARLIC, CRUSHED

1 TABLESPOON EXTRA VIRGIN OLIVE OIL

1 SMALL RED ONION (100G), CUT INTO THIN WEDGES

3 MEDIUM HEIRLOOM TOMATOES (450G),
QUARTERED

25G (¾ OUNCE) BABY ROCKET (ARUGULA) LEAVES

½ CUP (100G) MARINATED SOFT GOAT'S CHEESE,
RESERVE 2 TABLESPOONS OF THE
MARINATING OIL (SEE TIPS)

SPINACH PESTO DRESSING

½ CUP (130G) BABY SPINACH PESTO (SEE TIPS)

¼ CUP (60ML) EXTRA VIRGIN OLIVE OIL

1 Combine lamb, garlic and oil in a medium bowl; season with black pepper and sea salt.

2 Cook onion on a heated oiled grill plate (or pan or barbecue) until browned and just tender; season to taste. Cover loosely with foil to keep warm.

3 Cook lamb on heated oiled grill plate (or pan or barbecue), turning occasionally, for 10 minutes for medium or until cooked as desired. Stand, covered loosely with foil, for 5 minutes. Slice thickly.

4 Meanwhile, make spinach pesto dressing.

5 Place onion, tomato, rocket and reserved marinating oil in a large bowl; toss gently to combine. Season to taste.

6 Add lamb to salad; toss to combine. Arrange salad on a platter. Top with crumbled cheese; drizzle with dressing.

SPINACH PESTO DRESSING Place ingredients in a small screw-top jar; shake well. Season to taste.

mediterranean grain salad with honey-cumin labne

SERVES 6

Wholegrains, such as the brown rice and quinoa in this recipe, are great plant sources of protein and fibre, as well as a host of vitamins, minerals, and phytochemicals that improve your health. Seeds and nuts are also great sources of vitamins and minerals, as well as omega-3 fats.

TIPS Toast/roast all nuts and seeds together on an oven tray (place the cumin seeds and flaked almonds on small pieces of foil to keep them separate), in a preheated 180°C/350°F oven for 8 minutes, stirring halfway through cooking time. Labne is yoghurt that has been drained of whey. Draining for a short time results in a thick, creamy yoghurt, while longer draining achieves the consistency of a soft yoghurt cheese that can be rolled into balls. It is available from major supermarkets.

PREP + COOK TIME 45 MINUTES

¾ CUP (150G) BROWN RICE

½ CUP (100G) FRENCH-STYLE GREEN LENTILS, RINSED

½ CUP (100G) RED QUINOA

1 CUP (250ML) WATER

1 SMALL RED ONION (100G), CHOPPED FINELY

2 TABLESPOONS PEPITAS (PUMPKIN SEED KERNELS),
 TOASTED (SEE TIPS)

2 TABLESPOONS SUNFLOWER SEED KERNELS,
 TOASTED (SEE TIPS)

2 TABLESPOONS PINE NUTS, TOASTED (SEE TIPS)

2 TABLESPOONS BABY CAPERS

½ CUP (80G) CURRANTS

1 CUP FRESH FLAT-LEAF PARSLEY LEAVES

1 CUP FRESH CORIANDER (CILANTRO) LEAVES

¼ CUP (60ML) LEMON JUICE

⅓ CUP (80ML) EXTRA VIRGIN OLIVE OIL

1 TEASPOON CUMIN SEEDS, TOASTED (SEE TIPS)

1 CUP (280G) LABNE (SEE TIPS)

1½ TABLESPOONS HONEY

½ CUP (40G) FLAKED ALMONDS, TOASTED (SEE TIPS)

1 Cook rice and lentils in separate large saucepans of boiling water for 25 minutes or until tender; drain, rinse well.

2 Place quinoa in a small saucepan with the water, bring to the boil. Reduce heat to low; cook, covered, for 10 minutes or until tender. Drain.

3 Place rice, lentils and quinoa in a large bowl. Add onion, seeds, pine nuts, capers, currants, herbs, lemon juice and oil; stir until well combined.

4 Combine cumin seeds and labne in a small bowl; drizzle with honey.

5 Divide salad among six plates; top with spoonfuls of labne. Sprinkle with almonds.

za'atar chickpea & roast vegetable salad

SERVES 4

Za'atar can be used to 'spice up' a variety of simple dishes. Spread slices of sourdough or pieces of pitta bread with olive oil and then sprinkle with a generous amount of za'atar as an easy snack or starter when entertaining. Or sprinkle the spice mix over Greek-style yoghurt and drizzle with olive oil for an accompaniment to fish or chicken, or as a creamy dip with crackers.

TIPS Rainbow baby carrots are also sold as heirloom carrots; they are available from major supermarkets and greengrocers. Za'atar is a Middle-Eastern spice mixture usually containing sesame seeds, dried oregano (rigani) or dried thyme, sumac and sea salt. It is available in major supermarkets and Middle-Eastern food stores.

PREP + COOK TIME 45 MINUTES

**500G (1 POUND) BUTTERNUT PUMPKIN, PEELED,
   CUT INTO THIN WEDGES**

**1 LARGE RED ONION (300G), CUT INTO
   THIN WEDGES**

**1 MEDIUM RED CAPSICUM (BELL PEPPER) (200G),
   SLICED THICKLY**

**1 MEDIUM YELLOW CAPSICUM (BELL PEPPER) (200G),
   SLICED THICKLY**

**400G (12½ OUNCES) RAINBOW BABY (DUTCH)
   CARROTS, TRIMMED (SEE TIPS)**

⅓ CUP (80ML) EXTRA VIRGIN OLIVE OIL

**400G (12½ OUNCES) CANNED CHICKPEAS
   (GARBANZO BEANS), DRAINED, RINSED**

2 TABLESPOONS ZA'ATAR (SEE TIPS)

¼ CUP (60ML) RED WINE VINEGAR

**60G (2 OUNCES) RED VEINED SORREL OR
   BABY SPINACH LEAVES**

100G (3 OUNCES) PERSIAN FETTA, CRUMBLED

⅓ CUP SMALL FRESH MINT LEAVES

1 Preheat oven to 220°C/425°F. Line two large oven trays with baking paper.

2 Place pumpkin, onion, capsicum and carrots, in a single layer, on one oven tray; drizzle with 2 teaspoons oil. Season. Roast for 25 minutes or until vegetables are tender.

3 Meanwhile, place chickpeas on remaining tray. Drizzle with 2 teaspoons oil, sprinkle with za'atar; toss gently to coat. Roast for 25 minutes or until golden and crisp.

4 For the dressing, whisk vinegar and remaining oil in a small bowl; season to taste.

5 Combine vegetables, chickpeas, leaves, fetta and mint in four bowls; drizzle with dressing. Season to taste.

mint lamb skewers with garlic beans & tzatziki

SERVES 4

Tzatziki is a traditional Greek sauce that is served with grilled meats, especially strongly flavoured proteins such as lamb or goat, or served as dip on its own. It is readily available from most major supermarkets, but we prefer to make our own as to avoid any hidden sugars or additives.

TIPS Run a teaspoon down the centre of the cucumber to remove the seeds. If you use bamboo skewers, soak them for 10 minutes in boiling water before using to prevent them burning during cooking.

PREP + COOK TIME 45 MINUTES

2 CLOVES GARLIC, QUARTERED

½ CUP FRESH MINT LEAVES

½ TEASPOON CRACKED BLACK PEPPER

½ TEASPOON SEA SALT FLAKES

1 TABLESPOON EXTRA VIRGIN OLIVE OIL

8 LAMB FILLETS (550G)

GARLIC BEANS

400G (12½ OUNCES) GREEN BEANS, TRIMMED

2 TABLESPOONS EXTRA VIRGIN OLIVE OIL

1 CLOVE GARLIC, SLICED THINLY

2 TABLESPOONS PINE NUTS, TOASTED

TZATZIKI DRESSING

1 LEBANESE CUCUMBER (130G),
    HALVED LENGTHWAYS

2 TABLESPOONS LEMON JUICE

1 CLOVE GARLIC, CRUSHED

1 CUP (280G) GREEK-STYLE YOGHURT

1 Pound garlic, mint, pepper and salt using a mortar and pestle until mixture resembles a thick paste. Stir in oil.

2 Thread lamb onto eight 25cm (10-inch) metal skewers. Place lamb skewers in a shallow glass or ceramic dish, add mint mixture; turn skewers to coat in mixture.

3 Make garlic beans, then tzatziki dressing.

4 Cook lamb on a heated oiled grill plate (or pan or barbecue), turning occasionally, for 10 minutes for medium or until cooked as desired.

5 Serve lamb with garlic beans and tzatziki dressing.

GARLIC BEANS Boil, steam or microwave beans until just tender; drain. Refresh in a large bowl of iced water; drain. Halve lengthways; place in a large bowl. Place oil and garlic in a small frying pan over low heat; cook until garlic is golden. Add pine nuts; stir until lightly golden. Drizzle mixture over beans.

TZATZIKI DRESSING Remove and discard seeds from cucumber (see tips); coarsely grate flesh. Combine with remaining ingredients in a medium bowl; season to taste.

Weeknight
Dinners

roasted sumac chicken with baby vegetables

SERVES 4

This roast chicken makes the perfect family dinner, with any leftovers great for salads and sandwiches the next day. Sumac is a purple-red, astringent spice ground from berries growing on shrubs that flourish wild around the Mediterranean; it adds a tart, lemony flavour to dips and dressings, and goes well with barbecued meats.

TIP Use goat's fetta or ricotta instead of regular fetta, if you prefer.

PREP + COOK TIME 1 HOUR 15 MINUTES

30G (1 OUNCE) BUTTER, SOFTENED

1 TABLESPOON SUMAC

1.4KG (2¾-POUND) CHICKEN

500G (1 POUND) BABY BEETROOT (BEETS), TRIMMED

250G (8 OUNCES) BABY (DUTCH) CARROTS, TRIMMED

250G (8 OUNCES) YELLOW BABY (DUTCH) CARROTS, TRIMMED

1 TABLESPOON EXTRA VIRGIN OLIVE OIL

½ CUP FRESH MINT LEAVES

100G (3 OUNCES) GREEK FETTA, CRUMBLED (SEE TIP)

2 TABLESPOONS PISTACHIO DUKKAH

1 Preheat oven to 180°C/350°F.

2 Combine butter and sumac in a small bowl. Rub sumac butter all over the outside of the chicken; season. Tie chicken legs together with kitchen string; place in a large roasting pan. Wrap beetroot individually in foil; add to pan with chicken. Roast for 30 minutes.

3 Baste chicken with pan juices. Toss carrots in oil; season and add to pan. Roast a further 35 minutes or until chicken is cooked through and skin is golden brown. Cover chicken loosely with foil; stand for 10 minutes.

4 Meanwhile, peel beetroot and cut in half. Return beetroot to pan.

5 Serve roast chicken and vegetables with mint, fetta and dukkah.

French-style lamb & lentil salad

SERVES 6

Lamb backstrap comes from the back of the animal near the spine, trimmed from the middle of the loin. This cut is free from fat, gristle and bone. In contrast to other cuts of lamb, backstrap is wonderfully lean and meaty, which lends itself to being panfried, or sliced and stir-fried.

TIP White balsamic vinegar is available from supermarkets. You can use white wine vinegar or lemon juice instead.

PREP + COOK TIME 40 MINUTES

1½ CUPS (300G) DRIED FRENCH-STYLE GREEN LENTILS, RINSED

750G (1½ POUNDS) LAMB BACKSTRAPS (EYE OF LOIN)

1 TABLESPOON EXTRA VIRGIN OLIVE OIL

2 TEASPOONS GROUND CUMIN

350G (11 OUNCES) BABY GREEN BEANS, TRIMMED

1 SMALL RED ONION (100G), SLICED THINLY

100G (3 OUNCES) WATERCRESS SPRIGS

200G (6½ OUNCES) SOFT GOAT'S CHEESE, CRUMBLED

WHITE BALSAMIC DRESSING

1 CLOVE GARLIC, CRUSHED

¼ CUP (60ML) WHITE BALSAMIC VINEGAR (SEE TIP)

¼ CUP (60ML) EXTRA VIRGIN OLIVE OIL

1 TABLESPOON DIJON MUSTARD

2 TEASPOONS CASTER (SUPERFINE) SUGAR

1 Cook lentils in a large saucepan of boiling water for 20 minutes or until tender; drain.

2 Meanwhile, make white balsamic dressing.

3 Combine lentils with half the dressing in a large bowl.

4 Cook lamb on a heated oiled grill plate (or pan or barbecue), brushing frequently with combined oil and cumin, for 4 minutes on each side or until cooked as desired. Stand, covered loosely with foil, for 5 minutes.

5 Meanwhile, boil, steam or microwave beans until tender; drain. Refresh under cold running water; drain well.

6 Add beans, onion, watercress, cheese and half the remaining dressing to lentils; toss gently to combine. Slice lamb thickly.

7 Serve lentil salad topped with lamb; drizzle with remaining dressing.

WHITE BALSAMIC DRESSING Whisk ingredients in a small bowl until combined; season to taste.

chicken, burghul & pomegranate salad

SERVES 6

Since ancient times, pomegranates have been cultivated in the Mediterranean; its bright red arils, the seeds of the fruit, feature heavily in the art, poetry and myths of the region, as well as in the cuisine.

TIPS Pomegranate molasses is available from delis, Middle-Eastern food stores, specialty food shops and most major supermarkets. Burghul (cracked wheat) can be bought from health food stores. To remove seeds from the pomegranate, cut it in half crossways; hold one half at a time, cut-side down, in the palm of your hand over a bowl, then hit the outside firmly with a wooden spoon. The seeds should fall out easily; discard any white pith that falls out with them.

PREP + COOK TIME 45 MINUTES (+ REFRIGERATION & STANDING)

¼ CUP (60ML) EXTRA VIRGIN OLIVE OIL

¼ CUP (60ML) POMEGRANATE MOLASSES (SEE TIPS)

1 TABLESPOON GROUND CUMIN

2 CLOVES GARLIC, CRUSHED

1KG (2 POUNDS) CHICKEN BREAST FILLETS

1½ CUPS (375ML) CHICKEN STOCK

1½ CUPS (240G) FINE BURGHUL (SEE TIPS)

1 SMALL CAULIFLOWER (1KG)

1 LARGE POMEGRANATE (430G), SEEDS REMOVED (SEE TIPS)

1 MEDIUM RED ONION (170G), HALVED, SLICED THINLY

1 CUP FRESH FLAT-LEAF PARSLEY LEAVES

1 CUP (110G) COARSELY CHOPPED WALNUTS, ROASTED

150G (4½ OUNCES) GREEK FETTA, CRUMBLED

POMEGRANATE DRESSING

¼ CUP (60ML) EXTRA VIRGIN OLIVE OIL

¼ CUP (60ML) LEMON JUICE

3 TEASPOONS HONEY

3 TEASPOONS POMEGRANATE MOLASSES

1 Combine half the oil, the molasses, cumin and garlic in a large bowl; add chicken and turn to coat. Cover; refrigerate for 3 hours or overnight.

2 Bring stock to the boil in a medium saucepan. Remove from heat, add burghul; cover, stand for 5 minutes.

3 Meanwhile, preheat grill (broiler). Trim cauliflower; cut into 1.5cm (¾-inch) florets. Place on an oven tray; drizzle with remaining oil, season. Grill cauliflower for 8 minutes, turning halfway through cooking time, or until tender.

4 Make pomegranate dressing.

5 Drain chicken; discard marinade. Cook chicken on a heated oiled grill plate (or pan or barbecue) for 4 minutes on each side or until cooked through. Stand, covered loosely with foil, for 10 minutes. Slice thickly.

6 Spoon burghul onto a platter or bowl; top with chicken, cauliflower and remaining ingredients. Drizzle with dressing.

POMEGRANATE DRESSING Place ingredients in a screw-top jar; shake well. Season to taste.

pea & barley risotto with garlic prawns

SERVES 4

Risotto is traditionally made using a short-grain rice such as carnaroli or arborio, but here we use barley, a nutritious cereal grain that is higher in fibre than processed white rice. Soluble fibre has been shown to lower levels of blood cholesterol, a risk factor for cardiovascular diseases, while also improving the regulation of blood sugar. However, unlike rice, barley is not gluten-free.

TIP Risotto is best made just before serving.

PREP + COOK TIME 1 HOUR

¼ CUP (60ML) EXTRA VIRGIN OLIVE OIL

1 FRESH LONG RED CHILLI, CHOPPED FINELY

4 CLOVES GARLIC, CHOPPED FINELY

2 SHALLOTS (50G), CHOPPED FINELY

1 CUP (200G) PEARL BARLEY

1 LITRE (4 CUPS) CHICKEN STOCK

1 CUP (250ML) WATER

1 TABLESPOON FINELY GRATED LEMON RIND

½ CUP (60G) FROZEN PEAS

150G (4½ OUNCES) SUGAR SNAP PEAS, TRIMMED, HALVED LENGTHWAYS

400G (12½ OUNCES) UNCOOKED PEELED MEDIUM KING PRAWNS (SHRIMP)

EXTRA FINELY GRATED LEMON RIND, TO SERVE

1 Heat 1 tablespoon oil in a large heavy-based saucepan over low-medium heat, add chilli, half the garlic and shallot; cook, stirring, for 3 minutes or until tender. Add barley; cook, stirring for 2 minutes or until lightly toasted. Add half the stock; bring to the boil. Reduce heat to low; cook, stirring occasionally, for 18 minutes or until the liquid has been absorbed. Add remaining stock and the water; cook, stirring occasionally, for a further 18 minutes or until most of the liquid has been absorbed. Add rind, peas and sugar snap peas; cook, stirring, for 3 minutes or until vegetables are tender. Season to taste.

2 Meanwhile, shell and devein prawns, leaving tails intact. Heat remaining oil in a medium frying pan over high heat; cook prawns and remaining garlic, stirring, for 5 minutes or until prawns are just cooked. Season.

3 Divide risotto among four bowls; top with prawns and extra lemon rind.

pan-fried whiting with tomato & olive salsa

SERVES 6

Eating a wide variety of seafood has a range of health benefits. Fish contain a large array of vitamins and minerals including vitamins A and D, phosphorus, magnesium, and selenium. Omega-3 fatty acids, found abundantly in seafood, are essential for our healthy development, and have been shown to help protect against heart disease and strokes.

DO-AHEAD
The salsa can be partially prepared up to a day ahead; add the parsley, remaining oil and lemon juice just before you cook the fish.

PREP + COOK TIME 50 MINUTES

1KG (2 POUNDS) KIPFLER (FINGERLING) POTATOES, HALVED LENGTHWAYS

2 TABLESPOONS RED WINE VINEGAR

¼ CUP (60ML) EXTRA VIRGIN OLIVE OIL

400G (12½ OUNCES) GREEN BEANS, TRIMMED

½ CUP (75G) PLAIN (ALL-PURPOSE) FLOUR

12 X 80G (2½-OUNCE) WHITING FILLETS, SKIN ON

LEMON WEDGES, TO SERVE

TOMATO & OLIVE SALSA

⅓ CUP (80ML) EXTRA VIRGIN OLIVE OIL

2 CLOVES GARLIC, CRUSHED

500G (1 POUND) GRAPE TOMATOES, HALVED

150G (4½ OUNCES) KALAMATA OLIVES

½ SMALL RED ONION (50G), CHOPPED FINELY

½ CUP FRESH FLAT-LEAF PARSLEY LEAVES

2 TABLESPOONS LEMON JUICE

1 Make tomato and olive salsa.

2 Place potatoes in a large saucepan, cover with cold water; bring to the boil. Boil for 8 minutes or until tender; drain. Transfer to a large bowl; drizzle with vinegar and 1 tablespoon of the oil. Cover to keep warm.

3 Meanwhile, cook green beans in a saucepan of boiling water for 3 minutes or until tender; drain. Refresh in a bowl of iced water; drain. Add to potatoes in bowl; toss gently to combine.

4 Season flour with salt and pepper; coat fish in seasoned flour, shake off excess. Heat remaining oil in a large frying pan over medium heat; cook fish, skin-side down, in batches, for 1½ minutes or until skin crisps. Turn, cook for a further 1 minute or until fish is just cooked through.

5 Divide potato and beans among plates; top with fish and salsa. Serve with lemon wedges.

TOMATO & OLIVE SALSA Heat 1 tablespoon oil in a medium saucepan over medium heat; cook garlic, stirring, until fragrant. Stir in tomatoes and olives; cook until heated through. Remove from heat; stir in onion, parsley, remaining oil and the juice. Season to taste.

salmon parcels with kipfler potatoes

SERVES 2

After tuna, salmon might be the most popular fish in the world to eat. Luckily when baked, panfried or grilled, salmon is also among the most heart-healthy of fish. It is packed with vitamins and minerals, such as B12, vitamin D and selenium, and is a good source of niacin, omega-3 fatty acids, protein, phosphorus and potassium.

TIPS Baking the salmon in a parcel locks in all the flavours, juices and steam to give a moist and flavoursome result. You could try using firm white fish fillets or even chicken breast instead of salmon. The cooking time will vary depending on the thickness of the cut.

PREP + COOK TIME 50 MINUTES

300G (9½ OUNCES) KIPFLER (FINGERLING)
POTATOES, SLICED THINLY

1 SMALL RED ONION (100G), CUT INTO THIN WEDGES

1 TABLESPOON EXTRA VIRGIN OLIVE OIL

½ MEDIUM LEMON (70G), SLICED THINLY

1 SMALL TOMATO (90G), SLICED THINLY

2 X 180G (5½-OUNCE) SKINLESS BONELESS
SALMON FILLETS

2 TEASPOONS BABY CAPERS

1 TEASPOON FENNEL SEEDS

100G (3 OUNCES) BABY SPINACH LEAVES

¼ CUP FRESH FLAT-LEAF PARSLEY LEAVES

1 Preheat oven to 200°C/400°F.

2 Combine potato and onion in a roasting pan; drizzle with half the oil. Roast for 30 minutes or until browned lightly and tender.

3 Meanwhile, arrange lemon and tomato on two 30cm (12-inch) square pieces of baking paper. Top with salmon, capers and fennel seeds; drizzle with remaining oil. Fold paper into a parcel to enclose salmon; place on an oven tray. Bake for 8 minutes or until salmon is cooked as desired.

4 Serve salmon parcels with potato and onion; top with spinach and parsley.

barbecued calamari with lemon cracked wheat risotto

SERVES 2

Burghul is used extensively in Middle-Eastern cuisine, but is also eaten widely throughout the Mediterranean region. Eaten as you would rice or couscous, burghul has a course texture and nutty flavour, and can be used in soups, stews and salads, such as tabbouleh. Burghul is low in fat, high in minerals like manganese, magnesium and iron, plus is a good source of plant-based protein.

TIPS If you want to clean your own calamari you will need 850g (1½ pounds) whole calamari. For details on how to clean calamari, see Glossary, page 235. You could also try this with thin strips of chicken or pork. Burghul (cracked wheat) can be bought from health food stores. Serve with baby rocket (arugula) leaves, if you like.

PREP + COOK TIME 45 MINUTES

300G (9½ OUNCES) CLEANED SMALL CALAMARI HOODS, HALVED (SEE TIPS)

3 CLOVES GARLIC, CRUSHED

2 TEASPOONS CHOPPED FRESH OREGANO LEAVES

1 TEASPOON FINELY GRATED LEMON RIND

1 TABLESPOON EXTRA VIRGIN OLIVE OIL

1 SMALL ONION (80G), CHOPPED FINELY

2 TEASPOONS FRESH LEMON THYME LEAVES

½ CUP (80G) COARSE BURGHUL

2 CUPS (500ML) WATER

1 CUP (120G) FROZEN PEAS

1 TABLESPOON LEMON JUICE

2 TEASPOONS FRESH OREGANO LEAVES, EXTRA

1 Using a sharp knife, score inside surface of calamari in a criss-cross pattern at 1cm (½-inch) intervals. Cut into 4cm (1½-inch) strips. Place in a bowl with 1 garlic clove, chopped oregano, lemon rind and 2 teaspoons of the oil; stir to combine.

2 Heat remaining oil in a medium non-stick frying pan over medium heat; cook onion, remaining garlic and the thyme, stirring, for 5 minutes or until onion is softened.

3 Add burghul and the water; cook, stirring occasionally, for 15 minutes or until burghul is tender. Add peas and lemon juice; cook, stirring, for 2 minutes or until heated through.

4 Meanwhile, cook calamari on a heated grill plate (or pan or barbecue), turning halfway through cooking time, for 2 minutes or until just cooked through.

5 Serve calamari with burghul mixture; sprinkle with extra oregano.

lamb kofta with zucchini baba ganoush

SERVES 4

Traditionally baba ganoush is a dish consisting of a mixture of smoky eggplant, tahini, olive oil and various spices. In our version we have replaced the eggplant with roasted zucchini for a fresh, lighter take on the classic. Tahini is a paste made from toasted hulled sesame seeds and is available from most major supermarkets and Middle-Eastern food stores.

TIP Chilling the food processor bowl and blade in the freezer for 15 minutes before processing the kofta mixture ensures the mixture is nicely chopped and not mushy.

PREP + COOK TIME 1 HOUR 15 MINUTES (+ REFRIGERATION)

600G (1¼ POUNDS) BONELESS LAMB LEG MEAT, CHOPPED COARSELY

1 EGG

2 TEASPOONS GROUND CUMIN

1 CLOVE GARLIC, CRUSHED

¾ CUP FINELY CHOPPED FRESH MINT LEAVES

1 MEDIUM LEMON (140G)

1 CUP (200G) PEARL BARLEY

3 CUPS (750ML) WATER

1½ CUPS (180G) FROZEN PEAS

⅓ CUP (80ML) EXTRA VIRGIN OLIVE OIL

MINT LEAVES, EXTRA, TO SERVE

ZUCCHINI BABA GANOUSH

2 LARGE ZUCCHINI (300G), UNTRIMMED

1½ TABLESPOONS EXTRA VIRGIN OLIVE OIL

1 TABLESPOON TAHINI

½ TEASPOON GROUND CUMIN

1 SMALL CLOVE GARLIC, CRUSHED

1 Process lamb, egg, cumin and garlic in a food processor until finely chopped. Place in a large bowl with ¼ cup of chopped mint. Season and knead for 2 minutes or until well combined. Divide mixture into 8 portions. Shape portions into koftas. Press onto skewers. Refrigerate for 1 hour.

2 Meanwhile, finely grated rind from lemon. Squeeze juice; reserve 1½ tablespoons juice for zucchini baba ganoush.

3 Make zucchini baba ganoush.

4 Place barley and the water in a medium saucepan, bring to the boil. Reduce heat to low; cook, covered, for 35 minutes or until tender. Drain. Cook peas in a saucepan of boiling water for 2 minutes or until tender; drain.

5 Place barley, peas, remaining chopped mint and 2 tablespoons oil in a large bowl; toss gently to combine. Season to taste.

6 Brush kofta with remaining oil; cook on a heated grill plate (or barbecue) over medium-high heat, turning, for 10 minutes or until cooked as desired.

7 Serve kofta with baba ganoush and barley salad, sprinkled with mint.

ZUCCHINI BABA GANOUSH Preheat oven to 220°C/425°F. Bake whole zucchini on an oven tray for 40 minutes or until very soft and slightly blackened. Process zucchini with oil, tahini, cumin, garlic and reserved lemon juice. Season to taste.

barbecued salmon with chermoulla sauce

SERVES 6

Chermoulla is a traditional Moroccan spice rub typically used to flavour fish or seafood; swirled through Greek-style yoghurt, it makes a delicious sauce to accompany the barbecued salmon and vegetables in this recipe. This sauce would also work well with red meat, other seafood and drizzled over roasted vegetables; make double and keep it in the fridge to add flavour to simple dishes.

TIPS Serve the salmon fillets whole, if preferred. Sprinkle with fresh coriander (cilantro) leaves before serving, if you like.

PREP + COOK TIME 30 MINUTES

2 MEDIUM RED ONIONS (340G)

3 MEDIUM ZUCCHINI (360G), SLICED THINLY, LENGTHWAYS

340G (11 OUNCES) ASPARAGUS, TRIMMED

¼ CUP (60ML) EXTRA VIRGIN OLIVE OIL

6 X 180G (5½-OUNCE) SALMON FILLETS, SKIN ON

LEMON WEDGES, TO SERVE

CHERMOULLA SAUCE

½ CUP FIRMLY PACKED FRESH FLAT-LEAF PARSLEY LEAVES

½ CUP FIRMLY PACKED FRESH CORIANDER (CILANTRO) LEAVES

2 CLOVES GARLIC, CHOPPED COARSELY

1 TEASPOON DRIED CHILLI FLAKES

1 TEASPOON GROUND CUMIN

1 TEASPOON GROUND CORIANDER

½ TEASPOON GROUND TURMERIC

1 TABLESPOON LEMON JUICE

1 TABLESPOON EXTRA VIRGIN OLIVE OIL

½ CUP (140G) GREEK-STYLE YOGHURT

1 Make chermoulla sauce.

2 Cut each onion into 8 wedges, keeping root ends intact. Combine onion, zucchini and asparagus with 1 tablespoon of the oil in a medium bowl.

3 Cook vegetables on a heated oiled grill plate (or pan or barbecue) until charred and tender. Cover loosely with foil to keep warm.

4 Rub fish with another tablespoon of oil; season. Cook fish, skin-side down, on heated oiled grill plate (or pan or barbecue) until skin crisps; turn, cook until just cooked through.

5 Top grilled vegetables with salmon, flaked into bite-sized pieces, and sauce; drizzle with remaining oil. Serve with lemon wedges.

CHERMOULLA SAUCE Blend or process herbs, garlic, chilli and ground spices until combined. Add juice and oil; process until smooth. Transfer to a medium bowl; stir in yoghurt. Season to taste.

roasted fish with celeriac & fennel salad

SERVES 8

Roasting a whole fish may seem intimidating, but there really is nothing to it, and they make an amazing impression when plated and served. Juniper berries are not true berries, but are instead seeds produced by the various species of juniper trees. Used as a spice in European cuisine, they also give gin its distinctive flavour. They are the only spice to be derived from conifers.

TIPS If you have a zester, use it to create strips of lemon rind. Alternatively, peel two long, wide strips of rind from the lemon, without the white pith, then cut into thin strips lengthways. Use a mandoline or V-slicer to quickly and easily cut the celeriac into fine matchsticks and the fennel into thin slices.

PREP + COOK TIME 1 HOUR (+ REFRIGERATION & STANDING)

8 WHOLE SMALL SNAPPER (2.6KG), CLEANED

8 THYME SPRIGS, TRIMMED

2 CLOVES GARLIC, SLICED THINLY

1 TABLESPOON DRIED JUNIPER BERRIES

¼ CUP (60ML) EXTRA VIRGIN OLIVE OIL

1 TABLESPOON FINELY GRATED LEMON RIND OR STRIPS (SEE TIPS)

LEMON WEDGES, TO SERVE

CELERIAC & FENNEL SALAD

700G (1½ POUNDS) CELERIAC (CELERY ROOT), PEELED, CUT INTO FINE MATCHSTICKS (SEE TIPS)

2 SMALL FENNEL BULBS (400G), TRIMMED, SLICED THINLY (SEE TIPS), FRONDS RESERVED

⅓ CUP FRESH FLAT-LEAF PARSLEY LEAVES

⅓ CUP (80ML) LEMON JUICE

¼ CUP (60ML) EXTRA VIRGIN OLIVE OIL

1 Wash fish inside and out, pat dry with paper towel. Season inside and out. Score fish twice through the thickest part on both sides. Place fish on an oven tray. Place a thyme sprig, some reserved fennel fronds and a slice of garlic into each cut. Using a mortar and pestle, grind juniper berries into a coarse powder. Coat fish all over with half the oil, rind and ground juniper berries. Refrigerate for 1 hour.

2 Meanwhile, make celeriac and fennel salad.

3 Preheat oven to 180°C/350°F. Line a large oven tray with baking paper.

4 Brush fish with remaining oil; place on lined tray. Roast fish for 18 minutes on until cooked through. Stand, covered loosely with foil, for 5 minutes.

5 Serve fish with salad and lemon cheeks.

CELERIAC & FENNEL SALAD Combine ingredients in a large bowl; season to taste.

The Spanish diet

Because of the great size of Spain as a country, its cuisine is extremely regional. The mountainous north experiences chilling winters so food is hearty and filling. Andalusia in the south has a warmer climate and much lighter food. With thousands of kilometres of coastline, parts of Spain, like Andalusia, are quintessentially Mediterranean. Plenty of tomatoes and capsicums, garlic, onions, beans, lentils and chickpeas, rice, good bread and liberal amounts of red wine characterise the traditional diet here. It's rich in fibre and antioxidants, derived from fresh herbs, olives and a repertoire of daily dishes based on seasonal produce. Low in saturated fats, fish is the main protein source and the range of seafood available is mind boggling. Andalusia is also amongst the world's largest producers of olive oil, which is the primary fat for much of Spain. Nuts, pasta, fruits and cheeses round out this diet. Studies show that Spain has the best life expectancy of any European country; interestingly, it is also one of the most steadfastly traditional of all European countries, in terms of its resistance to outside food influences. Spain is also a place where people don't obsess over kilojoules or low fat foods, but rather they eat what they enjoy, as part of a balanced intake.

Breakfast in the south is as often sweet, rich and deep-fried (churros served with thick hot chocolate) as it is light and savoury (tomato, Serrano ham and olive oil on toast is a staple) but the key is small portions. Lunch is the largest meal of the day; all over Spain, it's a three-course affair, usually starting with a soup or wedge of tortilla, followed by a meat, fish or rice dish (such as paella), then a light dessert like flan or fresh fruit. Valencia oranges are legendary, and many other fruits are grown and consumed in Spain – quince, strawberries, grapes, peaches and bananas among them. Drinking water and wine with meals is the Spanish habit, as is taking a few hours siesta to sleep off lunch. It's thought that this afternoon nap may also be an important contributor to the good health profile of the Spanish, as much as their overall eating habits. Dinners here are late and often amount to no more than a selection of snack-style tapas, eaten out. Made using cured meats, bread, fresh and preserved seafood, cheese, vegetables and preserves like olives, the tapas repertoire is huge and they're consumed with wine and in the company of friends. Boquerones, or white anchovies, are a tapas essential. Packed with omega-3 and omega-6 fatty acids, they're real stars of the Mediterranean diet.

Meat is enjoyed but often with restraint. Its presence in a meal might be confined to small amounts of chopped cured meats or sausages, fried with onion and garlic then used as a base for vegetable main dishes. During winter, heavier meals are commonly based around dried beans or chickpeas, especially long-cooked, simmered dishes such as cocido. These dishes incorporate meats but are equally amped up with hefty winter vegetables like squash, potatoes, onions, leeks, and garlic. Even in winter, a meal is preceded by a green salad, alongside which might be served baked capsicum stuffed with rice, some preserved white anchovies or flakes of tuna.

THE SPANISH LIFESTYLE

OLIVE OIL
Used liberally as a cooking medium and splashed over final dishes just before serving.

WATER & WINE
Most meals are consumed with wine – but usually only a glass or two, and drunk slowly.

EXCERCISE
The Spanish love to walk – they even have a specific verb, pasear, which means to "walk without a particular destination in mind."

FISH & SEAFOOD
Lots of fish, including preserved fish, is consumed. Canned tuna is so popular you can even buy it according to the cut.

FRUIT
Fresh fruit is the preferred dessert and is also eaten throughout the day as a snack.

WHOLEFOODS
Paella is wildly popular and is the perfect Mediterranean diet dish – it contains whole grains (rice), seafood or poultry, plenty of olive oil and vegetables.

ANTIOXIDANTS
Tomatoes and garlic, bursting with vitamins and powerful antioxidants, are intrinsic to the diet and are eaten in large quantities.

kale & spinach spanakopitas

MAKES 6

Spanakopita is known the world over. A family favourite, this fillo-crusted pie is eaten all across the regions of Greece. In rural areas the greens are often a mixture of spinach with leek, chard or sorrel. Here we also add the superfood kale, a nutritious leafy cabbage, for an extra nutrient boost.

TIPS You will need 2 bunches of silver beet and 1 bunch of green curly kale for this recipe. Trim the green onions so that they are 28cm (11¼ inches) long; discard the remainder of the tops. Serve with Greek-style yoghurt, if you like.

DO-AHEAD
You can make the spanakopitas up to the end of step 5, then put them into freezer bags and freeze for up to 1 month. Cook them from frozen, increasing the cooking time slightly or until the pastry is golden and the filling is heated through.

PREP + COOK TIME 1 HOUR 45 MINUTES

1.5KG (3 POUNDS) SILVER BEET (SWISS CHARD)

350G (11 OUNCES) GREEN CURLY KALE

400G (12½ OUNCES) GREEK FETTA, CRUMBLED

10 GREEN ONIONS (SCALLIONS), CHOPPED FINELY

½ CUP FINELY CHOPPED FRESH DILL

¾ CUP FINELY CHOPPED FRESH FLAT-LEAF PARSLEY

2 TEASPOONS FINELY GRATED LEMON RIND

¼ CUP (60ML) LEMON JUICE

3 EGGS, BEATEN LIGHTLY

80G (2½ OUNCES) BUTTER, MELTED

2 X 375G (12-OUNCE) PACKETS FRESH FILLO PASTRY

2 TEASPOONS SESAME SEEDS

LEMON WEDGES, TO SERVE

1 Preheat oven to 180°C/350°F.

2 Trim 4cm (1½-inches) off the stalks ends from silver beet and kale; discard. Rinse and drain greens, leaving some water clinging. Tear kale leaves from the centre stem. Cut white stalk from silver beet leaves, cutting into the leaf in a V-shape. Finely chop stems and leaves from greens, keeping them separate.

3 Heat a large heavy-based saucepan over high heat; cook stems, stirring occasionally, for 10 minutes or until softened. Drain well; transfer to a bowl.

Add chopped leaves to pan; cook for 2 minutes or until wilted. Drain well; add to bowl with stems. When cool enough to handle, squeeze excess water from greens mixture (this prevents the pies from becoming soggy).

4 Combine greens, fetta, green onion, herbs, rind, juice, and egg in a large bowl; season with freshly ground black pepper.

5 Butter six 2-cup (500ml), 18cm (7¼-inch) round, 3cm (1¼-inch) deep pie dishes. Butter half a sheet of pastry, fold in half to make a smaller rectangle; butter top. Place in dish, allowing pastry to overhang edge. Keep remaining sheets covered with baking paper topped with a clean, damp tea towel to prevent them from drying out. Repeat with two more sheets of pastry, stacking them in the dish. You will now have six layers. Place a sixth of the filling into the dish. Brush half a sheet of pastry with melted butter, fold in half crossways, brush with butter, fold in half again; trim to fit the top of the pie. Place over filling, then fold in and scrunch the overhanging pastry. Brush top of pie with a little more melted butter. Sprinkle with sesame seeds. Repeat to make six pies in total.

6 Sprinkle a little water over each pie; this will prevent the pastry from burning. Bake for 35 minutes or until golden. Serve spanakopitas with lemon wedges.

slow-roasted lamb shoulder with greek salad

SERVES 4

The long cooking time in this recipe ensures the lamb falls right off the bone. Start this dish on a cold Sunday morning or afternoon, so that your house fills with the delicious smell of the lamb as it roasts.

SERVING
SUGGESTION
You can serve the
lamb with the tzatziki
on page 158, if you like.

PREP + COOK TIME 4 HOURS

1.3KG (2¾-POUND) LAMB SHOULDER

2 TABLESPOONS EXTRA VIRGIN OLIVE OIL

1KG (2 POUNDS) POTATOES, SLICED THICKLY

2 MEDIUM ONIONS (300G), SLICED THINLY

4 DRAINED ANCHOVY FILLETS, CHOPPED FINELY

2 RED GARLIC BULBS (140G)

1 MEDIUM LEMON (140G), CUT INTO WEDGES

3 SPRIGS FRESH ROSEMARY

1 CUP (250ML) CHICKEN STOCK

1 CUP (250ML) WATER OR DRY WHITE WINE

GREEK SALAD

¼ CUP (60ML) EXTRA VIRGIN OLIVE OIL

1 TABLESPOON LEMON JUICE

1 TABLESPOON WHITE WINE VINEGAR

1 TABLESPOON FINELY CHOPPED FRESH OREGANO

1 CLOVE GARLIC, CRUSHED

3 MEDIUM TOMATOES (450G), CUT INTO WEDGES

2 LEBANESE CUCUMBERS (260G),
  CHOPPED COARSELY

200G (6½ OUNCES) GREEK FETTA, CRUMBLED

1 SMALL RED CAPSICUM (BELL PEPPER) (150G),
  SLICED THINLY

1 SMALL RED ONION (100G), SLICED THINLY

½ CUP (75G) PITTED BLACK OLIVES

1 Preheat oven to 180°C/350°F.

2 Season lamb. Heat the oil in a flameproof roasting pan over medium-high heat; cook lamb, turning, until browned all over. Remove from pan.

3 Layer potato, onion and anchovies in same pan; seasoning between layers. Cut garlic bulbs in half horizontally; place on vegetables with lemon wedges.

4 Place lamb on top of vegetable mixture; add rosemary. Pour combined stock and the water over vegetables. Cover pan tightly with two layers of foil. Roast for 1½ hours. Remove foil, reduce oven to 160°C/325°F; roast for a further 1½ hours or until the meat can be pulled from the bone easily. Transfer lamb to a tray. Stand, covered loosely with foil, for 20 minutes. Increase oven to 200°C/400°F.

5 Meanwhile, return vegetable mixture in pan to oven; roast for a further 20 minutes or until browned.

6 Make greek salad.

7 Serve lamb with roast vegetables and salad.

GREEK SALAD Whisk oil, juice, vinegar, oregano and garlic in a large bowl. Add remaining ingredients; toss gently to combine. Season to taste.

grilled sardines with pangrattato
SERVES 4

Pangrattato is Italian for breadcrumbs. In the sourthern parts of the country this crunchy bread topping was used as a substitute for the more expensive cheese. Recently it has become popular on its own merit as a delicious topping for vegetables, salads, and pasta, and makes a great addition to top crispy fried eggs. It is a perfect way to use up old, stale bread and save it from the bin.

TIPS Ask the fishmonger to clean the sardines for you. Serve with any salad leaves in your garden instead of watercress, if you like. Substitute the pine nuts with your favourite toasted nuts or seeds.

PREP + COOK TIME 20 MINUTES

750G (1½ POUNDS) FRESH SARDINES, CLEANED (SEE TIPS)

¼ CUP (60ML) EXTRA VIRGIN OLIVE OIL, PLUS EXTRA, FOR SERVING

1 MEDIUM LEMON (140G)

50G (1½ OUNCES) BABY ROCKET (ARUGULA) LEAVES

⅓ CUP WATERCRESS SPRIGS

¼ CUP (40G) PINE NUTS, TOASTED

PANGRATTATO

2 TABLESPOONS EXTRA VIRGIN OLIVE OIL

1 CUP (60G) COARSELY CHOPPED DAY-OLD BREAD

1 CLOVE GARLIC, CRUSHED

⅓ CUP COARSELY CHOPPED FRESH FLAT-LEAF PARSLEY

½ CUP (40G) FINELY GRATED PARMESAN

1 Make pangrattato.

2 Rub sardines with 2 tablespoons of the oil; season. Cook sardines on a heated grill plate (or pan or barbecue) over high heat for 2 minutes. Turn, cook for 1 minute or until cooked through.

3 Cut lemon in half; juice one half, cut remaining into wedges. Place rocket, watercress, pine nuts, juice and remaining oil in a medium bowl. Season.

4 Place rocket mixture on a platter; top with sardines, then drizzle with a little more oil. Sprinkle with pangrattato. Serve with lemon wedges.

PANGRATTATO Heat oil in a large frying pan over medium heat; cook bread, stirring, for 2 minutes or until golden. Add garlic; cook, stirring, for 1 minute or until fragrant. Cool for 10 minutes. Place in a food processor with parsley; pulse until coarse crumbs form. Stir in parmesan; season to taste.

beef souvlakia with fennel salad & garlic yoghurt

SERVES 4

There is nothing fancy about souvlakia, but there is something so comforting in these small pieces of meat cooked on skewers, with their smoky, grilled flavour and the pleasure of eating with your hands.

TIPS You can use bamboo skewers instead of rosemary skewers, if you like. Soak bamboo skewers for 10 minutes in boiling water before using to prevent them burning during cooking.

PREP + COOK TIME 40 MINUTES (+ REFRIGERATION)

1 MEDIUM LEMON (140G)

2 TABLESPOONS EXTRA VIRGIN OLIVE OIL

⅓ CUP (80ML) DRY WHITE WINE

1 TABLESPOON FINELY CHOPPED FRESH ROSEMARY

1 BAY LEAF, TORN

2 CLOVES GARLIC, CRUSHED

1KG (2 POUND) PIECE BEEF SIRLOIN OR RUMP,
    CUT INTO 4CM (1½-INCH) PIECES

8 ROSEMARY STALKS

GREEK PITTA BREAD, GRILLED, TO SERVE

FENNEL SALAD

2 MEDIUM FENNEL BULBS (600G)

2 TABLESPOONS EXTRA VIRGIN OLIVE OIL

1 TABLESPOON RED WINE VINEGAR

½ CUP (80G) MIXED PITTED OLIVES

GARLIC YOGHURT

1 CUP (280G) GREEK-STYLE YOGHURT

2 CLOVES GARLIC, CRUSHED

1 Finely grate rind from lemon. Remove white pith; coarsely chop flesh.

2 Combine oil, lemon rind and flesh, wine, chopped rosemary, torn bay leaf and garlic in a large non-reactive bowl; season. Add beef, toss to coat in mixture. Cover; refrigerate for 1 hour or overnight.

3 Make fennel salad, then garlic yoghurt.

4 Bring beef to room temperature. Evenly thread beef onto rosemary stalks.

5 Cook skewers, on a heated grill plate (or pan or barbecue) over medium-high heat, turning occasionally, for 5 minutes for medium rare or until cooked as desired.

6 Serve skewers with grilled pitta, fennel salad and garlic yoghurt.

FENNEL SALAD Trim the base of the fennel bulbs; reserve fronds. Using a mandoline or V-slicer, thinly slice fennel lengthways; place in a bowl of iced water. Drain well, lightly pat dry. Place fennel, half the reserved fennel fronds, oil, vinegar and olives in a medium bowl; toss well to combine. Season to taste.

GARLIC YOGHURT Place ingredients in a small bowl with remaining fennel fronds; stir to combine. Season to taste.

seafood & saffron stew

SERVES 4

A long held misconception is that if a mussel does not open when cooked, it should be discarded as it is 'bad'. This is a myth. As the molluscs are cooked, the heat softens the muscles that keep the shell together. If a mussel doesn't open during cooking, it is because the muscle hasn't softened sufficiently, but the mussel is actually fine to eat. Discard mussels that open before cooking and that smell bad.

TIPS If you want to clean your own calamari you will need 4 whole calamari; see Glossary, page 235. Ask your fishmonger to clean octopus for you. If you prefer, buy 1kg (2 pound) packs of pot-ready mussels from fishmongers or seafood markets. These are scrubbed, bearded and ready to cook. Some mussels might not open after cooking; do not discard but carefully pry open with a knife. For wide orange strips, use a vegetable peeler to peel strips and avoid taking off too much of the white pith with the rind as it is bitter. Serve with chargrilled bread, if you like.

PREP + COOK TIME 1 HOUR

4 CLEANED BABY CALAMARI HOODS (480G)
   (SEE TIPS)

250G (8 OUNCES) SMALL BLACK MUSSELS (SEE TIPS)

1 TABLESPOON EXTRA VIRGIN OLIVE OIL

2 MEDIUM ONIONS (300G), CHOPPED FINELY

2 CLOVES GARLIC, CRUSHED

3 WIDE STRIPS ORANGE RIND (SEE TIPS)

1 FRESH LONG RED CHILLI, CHOPPED FINELY

PINCH SAFFRON THREADS

⅓ CUP (80ML) DRY WHITE WINE

800G (1½ POUNDS) CANNED CRUSHED TOMATOES

1 LITRE (4 CUPS) FISH STOCK

1KG (2 POUNDS) UNCOOKED LARGE KING PRAWNS
   (SHRIMP), PEELED, DEVEINED, WITH TAILS INTACT

200G (6½ OUNCES) PIPIS, SCRUBBED

200G (6½ OUNCES) BABY OCTOPUS, CLEANED
   (SEE TIPS)

2 BABY FENNEL BULBS (260G)

2 TABLESPOONS LEMON JUICE

1 Using a sharp knife, slice calamari hoods crossways into 1cm (½-inch) rings. Scrub mussels; remove beards.

2 Heat oil in a large saucepan; cook onion, stirring, until soft. Add garlic; cook, stirring, for 1 minute.

3 Add rind, chilli, saffron and wine to onion mixture; cook, stirring, for 2 minutes. Add tomatoes; cook for 10 minutes or until mixture thickens slightly. Add stock; cook for 20 minutes or until liquid is reduced by about a quarter.

4 Add calamari, prawns, cleaned mussels, pipis and octopus to pan. Cook, covered, stirring occasionally, for 5 minutes or until seafood is just cooked.

5 Meanwhile, trim fennel; reserve fronds. Using a mandoline or V-slicer, cut fennel into very thin slices. Place fennel and juice in a small bowl; toss to coat well.

6 Serve stew topped with fennel mixture and reserved fennel fronds.

sweet & sour catalan silver beet with rosemary lamb

SERVES 4

Catalonia is a region in Northern Spain, with its own distinct language and culture. The colder weather of this region is reflected in this hearty sweet and sour dish, given its unique flavour by the combination of piquant sherry vinegar and sweet honey. You could serve the silver beet with any protein of your choice, grilled steak, pork or chicken, barbecued fish or seafood.

TIPS Wash silver beet well before using. You can use kale or cavolo nero (tuscan cabbage) instead of the silver beet, if you prefer.

DO-AHEAD Recipe can be prepared to the end of step 2 a day ahead. Keep vinegar mixture refrigerated.

PREP + COOK TIME 45 MINUTES (+ REFRIGERATION)

2 TABLESPOONS COARSELY CHOPPED FRESH
   ROSEMARY LEAVES

1 CLOVE GARLIC, CRUSHED

⅓ CUP (80ML) EXTRA VIRGIN OLIVE OIL

12 FRENCH-TRIMMED LAMB CUTLETS (600G)

3 GREEN ONIONS (SCALLIONS), SLICED THICKLY

⅓ CUP (80ML) SHERRY VINEGAR

2 SPRIGS FRESH THYME

2 TABLESPOONS HONEY

¼ CUP (40G) CURRANTS

500G (1 POUND) SILVER BEET (SWISS CHARD),
   TRIMMED

¼ CUP (40G) PINE NUTS, TOASTED

2 GREEN ONIONS (SCALLIONS), EXTRA,
   SLICED THINLY LENGTHWAYS

1 Combine rosemary, garlic and 2 tablespoons of oil in a large bowl; season. Reserve 1 tablespoon of the oil mixture in a small bowl for serving; cover, refrigerate. Add cutlets to large bowl; turn to coat in marinade. Cover; refrigerate for 1 hour or overnight.

2 Heat 1 tablespoon of the remaining oil in a small saucepan over low heat; cook green onion, stirring occasionally, for 1 minute or until softened. Add vinegar and thyme; bring to the boil. Reduce heat to low; cook for 5 minutes or until vinegar is reduced by half. Discard thyme. Stir in honey and currants; cool

3 Separate silver beet leaves from stems. Chop stems coarsely; shred leaves coarsely. Heat remaining oil in a large deep frying pan over medium heat; cook silver beet stems for 3 minutes or until just softened. Add silver beet leaves; cook, stirring, for 3 minutes or until just wilted. Season to taste. Transfer to a platter, drizzle with vinegar mixture and sprinkle with pine nuts; cover loosely with foil.

4 Meanwhile, cook cutlets on a heated oiled grill plate (or pan or barbecue) over medium-high heat for 2 minutes on each side for medium or until cooked as desired.

5 Drizzle lamb with reserved oil mixture; serve with silver beet mixture. Top with extra green onion.

baked sardines with fig & pine nut stuffing

SERVES 6

Also known as pignoli, a pine nut is not actually a nut but a small, cream-coloured kernel from pine cones. Best roasted before use to bring out the flavour, they are an essential ingredient for pesto.

TIPS Ask your fishmonger to clean and butterfly the sardines, if you like. Italian vincotto, literally meaning 'cooked wine', is a condiment made from boiling down grape must (skins, seeds and stems) until thick and syrupy. It is available from selected supermarkets and delis. You can use balsamic glaze instead.

PREP + COOK TIME 1 HOUR

⅔ CUP (130G) CHOPPED DRIED FIGS

⅓ CUP (80ML) RED WINE VINEGAR

⅓ CUP (80ML) EXTRA VIRGIN OLIVE OIL

1 CUP (70G) COARSE DAY-OLD SOURDOUGH
   BREADCRUMBS

1 MEDIUM RED ONION (170G), CHOPPED FINELY

2 CLOVES GARLIC, CRUSHED

2 TEASPOONS FINELY GRATED LEMON RIND

2 TABLESPOONS FINELY CHOPPED
   FRESH ROSEMARY

2 TABLESPOONS FINELY CHOPPED
   FRESH FLAT-LEAF PARSLEY

2 TABLESPOONS PINE NUTS, TOASTED

1 TABLESPOON LEMON JUICE

12 FRESH SARDINES (660G), CLEANED, BUTTERFLIED,
   WITH HEAD AND TAILS INTACT (SEE TIPS)

2 TABLESPOONS FRESH ROSEMARY LEAVES, EXTRA

1 MEDIUM FENNEL BULB (300G), TRIMMED, SLICED,
   FRONDS RESERVED

1 MEDIUM RADICCHIO (200G), CUT INTO 12 WEDGES

2 TABLESPOONS VINCOTTO (SEE TIPS)

LEMON WEDGES, TO SERVE

1 Preheat oven to 200°C/400°F. Oil and line a roasting pan with baking paper.

2 Place figs and vinegar in a small saucepan over medium heat; bring to a simmer. Cook for 1 minute; remove pan from heat. Stand for 10 minutes or until the liquid is absorbed.

3 Meanwhile, heat 1 tablespoon oil in a large frying pan over medium heat; cook breadcrumbs, stirring, for 5 minutes or until golden. Remove from pan. Wipe pan clean with paper towel.

4 Heat another tablespoon of oil in same pan over medium heat; cook onion, stirring, for 5 minutes or until soft. Add garlic, rind and rosemary; cook, stirring, for 1 minute or until fragrant. Remove pan from heat; stir in parsley, breadcrumbs, pine nuts, soaked fig mixture and lemon juice. Season to taste.

5 Place sardines, in a single layer, in lined pan. Place a heaped tablespoon of the stuffing mixture in the inside of each sardine, fold sardines over to enclose filling. Top with any remaining stuffing mixture and extra rosemary; drizzle with 1 tablespoon oil. Season.

6 Bake sardines for 15 minutes or until sardines are just cooked.

7 Meanwhile, brush fennel and radicchio with remaining oil; season. Cook fennel on a heated grill plate (or pan or barbecue) over medium heat for 2 minutes on each side or until charred lightly; transfer to a platter. Cook radicchio wedges on same grill plate (or pan or barbecue) for 1 minute on each side or until charred lightly and tender. Add radicchio to fennel; drizzle with half the vincotto. Sprinkle with reserved fronds.

8 Drizzle sardines with remaining vincotto. Serve with grilled fennel and radicchio, and lemon wedges.

roasted rosemary pork, fennel & potatoes

SERVES 4

Fennel is a crunchy green vegetable slightly resembling celery that's eaten raw in salads; fried as an accompaniment; or used as an ingredient in soups and sauces. It is also the name given to the dried seeds of the plant which have a stronger licorice flavour. The Greek name for fennel is marathon and the place of the famous battle of Marathon literally means a plain with fennel.

TIPS You could replace the pork with chicken breasts. Sprinkle with fennel fronds and fresh oregano leaves before serving, if you like.

PREP + COOK TIME 1 HOUR 15 MINUTES (+ STANDING)

1 TABLESPOON FINELY CHOPPED FRESH ROSEMARY LEAVES

2 TEASPOONS FINELY CHOPPED FRESH OREGANO LEAVES

2 TEASPOONS FENNEL SEEDS

½ TEASPOON DRIED CHILLI FLAKES

⅓ CUP (80ML) EXTRA VIRGIN OLIVE OIL

4 SMALL FENNEL BULBS (800G), TRIMMED, QUARTERED

800G (1½ POUNDS) KIPFLER (FINGERLING) POTATOES, HALVED LENGTHWAYS

500G (1 POUND) PORK FILLET

LEMON WEDGES, TO SERVE

1 Preheat oven to 220°C/425°F.

2 Combine rosemary, oregano, fennel seeds, chilli and ¼ cup of the oil in a small bowl; season. Place fennel bulbs and potato in a large roasting pan. Drizzle with two-thirds of the rosemary mixture; toss to combine. Roast for 30 minutes.

3 Rub pork with remaining rosemary mixture. Heat remaining oil in a heavy-based frying pan over high heat. Add pork; cook, turning, for 5 minutes or until browned all over.

4 Stir potato and fennel bulbs; place pork on top of vegetables. Roast for 20 minutes or until pork is just cooked through. Stand pork, covered loosely with foil, for 5 minutes.

5 Cut pork into slices; serve with potato, fennel and lemon wedges.

paprika & cumin spiced roast chicken with chickpeas

SERVES 4

Paprika is a ground spice made from dried sweet red capsicum (bell pepper), with many grades and types available, including sweet, mild, smoked and hot. The hotter types are usually combined with ground chilli peppers or cayenne pepper. Originating in central Mexico, paprika was brought to Spain in the 16th century, and is often used to add color to many types of dishes as well as flavour.

TIP Chicken supremes are chicken breasts with the skin on and wing bone still attached. They are available from specialty poultry stores; you may need to order them in advance.

PREP + COOK TIME 45 MINUTES

4 CLOVES GARLIC, CRUSHED

1 TABLESPOON SMOKED PAPRIKA

1 TEASPOON CUMIN SEEDS

½ CUP (125ML) EXTRA VIRGIN OLIVE OIL

½ CUP (140G) GREEK-STYLE YOGHURT

4 X 200G (6½-OUNCE) CHICKEN BREAST SUPREMES (SEE TIP)

400G (12½ OUNCES) CANNED CHICKPEAS (GARBANZO BEANS), DRAINED, RINSED

400G (12½ OUNCES) SMALL CHERRY TRUSS TOMATOES

200G (6½ OUNCES) FIRM RICOTTA, BROKEN INTO LARGE CHUNKS

¼ CUP CORIANDER (CILANTRO) SPRIGS

¼ CUP FRESH FLAT-LEAF PARSLEY LEAVES

1 Preheat oven to 240°C/475°F. Line a large roasting pan with baking paper.

2 Combine garlic, paprika, cumin and ⅓ cup of oil in a small bowl. Reserve 2 teaspoons of the spice oil mixture in another bowl and combine it with yoghurt; season to taste. Cover yoghurt mixture; refrigerate until required.

3 Rub 2 tablespoons of the remaining spice oil mixture over chicken; season. Heat remaining olive oil in a large frying pan over high heat; cook chicken for 2 minutes each side or until browned. Transfer chicken to lined pan. Roast chicken for 10 minutes.

4 Reduce oven to 200°C/400°F. Combine chickpeas, tomatoes, ricotta and remaining spice oil mixture in a large bowl. Spoon chickpea mixture around chicken in pan; season. Roast for a further 15 minutes or until chicken is cooked through.

5 Serve chicken and chickpea mixture with yoghurt sauce, sprinkled with coriander and parsley.

linguine primavera & poached eggs

SERVES 4

Primavera refers to the season of spring in Romance languages; this pasta is cooked with the best produce that spring has to offer, fresh beans, asaparagus and peas, to make a light weeknight dinner.

TIPS You could use 1½ cups (225g) frozen broad (fava) beans instead of fresh, if you like. It is important to use the freshest free-range eggs you can find, as they will hold their shape while poaching.

PREP + COOK TIME 30 MINUTES

920G (1¾ POUNDS) FRESH BROAD (FAVA) BEANS
    IN THE POD (SEE TIPS)

100G (3 OUNCES) SNOW PEAS, TRIMMED

2 TEASPOONS SALT

500G (1 POUND) LINGUINE

¼ CUP (60ML) EXTRA VIRGIN OLIVE OIL

2 CLOVES GARLIC, SLICED THINLY

170G (5½ OUNCES) ASPARAGUS, TRIMMED, CUT INTO
    5CM (2-INCH) LENGTHS ON THE DIAGONAL

4 EGGS

1 TEASPOON FINELY GRATED LEMON RIND

2 TABLESPOONS LEMON JUICE

¼ CUP FRESH CHERVIL LEAVES

1 CUP (80G) FINELY GRATED PARMESAN

1 Cook broad beans in a large saucepan of boiling water for 2 minutes or until just tender. Remove beans with a slotted spoon. Refresh under cold running water; drain well. Add snow peas to same pan; cook for 30 seconds or until bright green. Remove snow peas with a slotted spoon. Refresh under cold running water; drain well. Remove grey skins from broad beans.

2 Return water to the boil; add salt. Cook pasta in boiling water until almost tender; drain, reserving ¼ cup of cooking water. Return pasta to pan.

3 Meanwhile, heat 1 tablespoon of the oil in a large frying pan over medium-high heat; cook garlic and asparagus, stirring, for 2 minutes or until tender. Stir in broad beans and snow peas. Remove from heat.

4 Half-fill a large frying pan with water; bring to the boil. Break one egg into a cup, then slide into the pan; repeat with remaining eggs. When all eggs are in pan, return water to the boil. Cover pan, turning off heat; stand for 4 minutes or until a light film of egg white sets over yolks. Remove eggs, one at a time, using a slotted spoon; place spoon on paper-towel-lined saucer briefly to blot up any poaching liquid.

5 Return vegetable mixture to heat, add remaining oil, pasta, reserved cooking water, lemon rind and juice; toss until heated through. Season to taste.

6 Divide linguine among four bowls or plates; top each with a poached egg, chervil and parmesan. Season with freshly ground black pepper.

fish with pine nuts, currants & cavolo nero

SERVES 4

This agro dolce (sweet and sour) Italian recipe uses currants and grapes for sweetness and vinegar for a sour note. Grapes contain powerful antioxidants known as polyphenols, which may slow or prevent many types of cancer. The resveratrol found in red wine famous for heart health is a type of polyphenol found in the skins of red grapes.

TIP While we used flathead fillets, you can use any other white-fleshed fish, such as sand whiting or snapper instead.

PREP + COOK TIME 25 MINUTES

⅓ CUP (80ML) EXTRA VIRGIN OLIVE OIL

1 MEDIUM RED ONION (170G), HALVED, SLICED THINLY

1 CUP (170G) SMALL RED GRAPES, HALVED IF LARGE

2 TABLESPOONS CURRANTS

300G (9½ OUNCES) CAVOLO NERO (TUSCAN CABBAGE), TRIMMED, CHOPPED COARSELY

¼ CUP (60ML) RED WINE VINEGAR

⅓ CUP (50G) PINE NUTS, TOASTED

8 FLATHEAD FILLETS (800G) (SEE TIP)

FRESH FLAT-LEAF PARSLEY SPRIGS, TO SERVE

1 Heat ¼ cup of the oil in a large deep frying pan over medium-high heat; cook onion for 4 minutes or until softened. Add grapes and currants; cook for 1 minute. Add cavolo nero and vinegar; cook, stirring, for 1 minute or until cavolo nero just wilts. Add pine nuts.

2 Heat remaining oil in a large frying pan over medium-high heat; cook fish, in two batches, for 1½ minutes on each side or until just cooked through.

3 Serve fish with cavolo nero mixture, sprinkled with parsley.

wholegrain pizza marinara

SERVES 4

Here we give you a healthy substitute for a lazy Friday night takeaway pizza, ditching the white flour and greasy cheese for low-fat seafood chilli marinara and crispy wholemeal crust.

TIP Ask your fishmonger to clean the octopus for you, if you prefer.

PREP + COOK TIME 45 MINUTES
(+ REFRIGERATION & STANDING)

8 UNCOOKED MEDIUM KING PRAWNS (SHRIMP)
(180G)

4 CLEANED BABY OCTOPUS (360G), HALVED
LENGTHWAYS (SEE TIP)

2 FRESH LONG RED CHILLIES, CHOPPED FINELY

2 CLOVES GARLIC, CRUSHED

2 TEASPOONS FINELY GRATED LEMON RIND

2 TABLESPOONS EXTRA VIRGIN OLIVE OIL

200G (6 ½ OUNCES) CHERRY TOMATOES, HALVED

50G (1 ½ OUNCES) BABY ROCKET (ARUGULA) LEAVES

1 TABLESPOON LEMON JUICE

LEMON WEDGES, TO SERVE

DOUGH

¼ CUP (45G) FINE BURGHUL (CRACKED WHEAT)

½ CUP (125ML) WARM WATER

½ TEASPOON CASTER (SUPERFINE) SUGAR

1 TEASPOON DRIED YEAST

⅔ CUP (100G) PLAIN (ALL-PURPOSE) FLOUR

⅔ CUP (100G) WHOLEMEAL PLAIN (ALL-PURPOSE)
FLOUR

1 Peel and devein prawns; place in a large bowl with octopus. Combine chilli, garlic, rind and oil in a bowl; season to taste. Place half the chilli mixture in a small bowl, cover; refrigerate. Add remaining chilli mixture to prawns and octopus; toss to coat in mixture. Cover; refrigerate for 1 hour.

2 Meanwhile, make dough. Preheat oven to 220°C/425°F. Lightly oil four large oven trays.

3 Divide dough into four. Roll each piece into a 15cm (6-inch) round; place on trays. Bake pizza bases, in batches, for 8 minutes or until partially cooked. Top with seafood mixture and tomato. Bake pizzas, in batches, for a further 10 minutes or until bases are crisp and seafood is just cooked. Drizzle with reserved chilli mixture.

4 Place rocket and lemon juice in a small bowl; toss gently to coat. Season to taste.

5 Top pizzas with rocket mixture; serve with lemon wedges.

DOUGH Place burghul in a heatproof bowl; cover with boiling water; stand, covered, for 30 minutes. Rinse under cold water; drain. Combine the warm water, sugar and yeast in a small jug, cover; stand in a warm place for 10 minutes or until frothy. Combine burghul and sifted flours in a medium bowl. Add yeast mixture; mix to a soft dough. Knead dough on a floured surface for 5 minutes or until smooth and elastic. Place dough in an oiled medium bowl. Cover; stand in a warm place for 45 minutes or until doubled in size.

mussels in chilli broth with freekeh

SERVES 4

Mussels, like most seafood, are high in omega-3 fatty acids, which have been linked to a wide variety of health benefits such as reduction in the risk of cancer and cardiovascular disease, the reduction of inflammatory conditions, such as arthritis, and improving brain funtion. They are also relatively low in kilojoules and fat, while high in protein, vitamins and minerals.

TIPS If you prefer, you can buy 1kg (2-pound) packs of bearded, pot-ready mussels from fishmongers or seafood markets. Some mussels might not open after cooking; these might need careful prompting with a knife. Freekeh is an ancient grain food made from roasted young green wheat; it is available at health food shops, some delicatessens and greengrocers.

PREP + COOK TIME 1 HOUR 35 MINUTES

1KG (2 POUNDS) BLACK MUSSELS (SEE TIPS)

1 CUP (250ML) DRY WHITE WINE

1 TABLESPOON EXTRA VIRGIN OLIVE OIL

1 MEDIUM ONION (150G), CHOPPED FINELY

2 STALKS CELERY (300G), TRIMMED, HALVED
    LENGTHWAYS, SLICED THINLY

400G (12½ OUNCES) BABY (DUTCH) CARROTS,
    TRIMMED, SLICED THINLY ON THE DIAGONAL

2 TABLESPOONS TOMATO PASTE

1 CUP (170G) WHOLEGRAIN GREEN-WHEAT FREEKEH
    (SEE TIPS)

½ TEASPOON DRIED CHILLI FLAKES

3 CUPS (750ML) FISH STOCK

COARSELY CHOPPED FRESH FLAT-LEAF PARSLEY,
    TO SERVE

LEMON WEDGES, TO SERVE

1 Scrub mussels; remove beards.

2 Bring wine to the boil in a large saucepan over medium-high heat. Add mussels; cook, covered, for 8 minutes or until mussels open (see tips). Drain mussels in a colander over a large heatproof bowl; reserve cooking liquid. Cover mussels loosely with foil to keep warm.

3 Heat oil in same pan over medium heat; cook onion, celery and carrot for 3 minutes or until onion softens. Add tomato paste, freekeh and chilli; cook, stirring, for 1 minute or until fragrant. Add stock and reserved cooking liquid; bring to the boil. Reduce heat to low; cook, partially covered, for 1 hour until freekeh is tender.

4 Add mussels to pan; cook for 2 minutes or until heated through.

5 Top mussel and freekeh mixture with parsley; serve with lemon wedges.

lamb kofta, white beans & beetroot tzatziki
SERVES 4

Beetroot, also known as red beets, are firm, round root vegetables, notable for their distinct red colour and earthy, sweet flavour. Beetroot is a good source of iron and folate. It also contains nitrates, betaine, magnesium and other antioxidants. More recent health claims suggest beetroot can help lower blood pressure, boost exercise performance and prevent dementia.

TIPS If you don't have metal skewers, thread kofta onto bamboo skewers which have been soaked in boiling water for 10 minutes to prevent them burning during cooking. Cooked or uncooked kofta can be frozen for up to 3 months; thaw in the fridge.

SERVING SUGGESTION Serve kofta with pan-fried lemon slices, if you like.

PREP + COOK TIME 40 MINUTES

400G (12½ OUNCES) CANNED BUTTER BEANS, DRAINED, RINSED

1 TABLESPOON LEMON JUICE

2 TABLESPOONS FRESH OREGANO LEAVES

2 TABLESPOONS EXTRA VIRGIN OLIVE OIL

½ CUP (35G) FRESH BREADCRUMBS

2 TABLESPOONS MILK

600G (1¼ POUNDS) MINCED (GROUND) LAMB

1 TEASPOON GROUND ALLSPICE

⅓ CUP COARSELY CHOPPED FRESH OREGANO, EXTRA

100G (3 OUNCES) GREEK FETTA, CRUMBLED

1 BABY COS LETTUCE, TRIMMED, LEAVES SEPARATED

BEETROOT TZATZIKI

200G (6½ OUNCES) BEETROOT (BEETS), PEELED, GRATED COARSELY

1 CUP (280G) GREEK-STYLE YOGHURT

2 TABLESPOONS CHOPPED FRESH MINT LEAVES

1 CLOVE GARLIC, CRUSHED

1 TABLESPOON FINELY GRATED LEMON RIND

1 Make beetroot tzatziki.

2 Combine butter beans, juice, oregano leaves and half the oil in a medium bowl; season to taste.

3 Place breadcrumbs and milk in a medium bowl; stand for 3 minutes or until milk has been absorbed. Add lamb, allspice and extra oregano; season. Using your hands, work mixture until well combined. Add fetta; mix until combined. Roll heaped tablespoonful measures of lamb mixture into ball shapes. Thread onto 8 skewers.

4 Heat remaining oil in a large non-stick frying pan over medium-high heat; cook kofta, turning occasionally, for 10 minutes or until browned and cooked through.

5 Serve kofta on lettuce with bean mixture and beetroot tzatziki.

BEETROOT TZATZIKI Combine ingredients in a medium bowl; season to taste.

vine-wrapped whiting with yoghurt tartare & sweet potato chips

SERVES 4

Grape vine leaves are used abudantly in Mediterranean food, most famously for the Greek dolmades, vine leaves stuffed with rice. These sweet potato chips make a delicious change from regular potatoes, higher in fibre and slightly lower on the glycemic index than their white counterparts, while also being packed with vitamins A, vitamins B5 and B6, and (due to their orange colour) high in carotenoids.

TIPS Preserved vine leaves are available from Middle-Eastern food stores and some delicatessens. You can use 8 whole, cleaned sardines instead of whiting, if you like.

PREP + COOK TIME 45 MINUTES

1KG (2 POUNDS) SMALL ORANGE SWEET POTATO, UNPEELED, CUT INTO CHIPS

6 SPRIGS FRESH OREGANO

2 TABLESPOONS EXTRA VIRGIN OLIVE OIL

8 WHOLE SAND WHITING (1KG), CLEANED

8 MEDIUM PRESERVED VINE LEAVES, RINSED

1 MEDIUM LEMON (140G), CUT INTO WEDGES

2 TABLESPOONS FRESH DILL

YOGHURT TARTARE

1 CUP (280G) GREEK-STYLE YOGHURT

1 TABLESPOON WHITE BALSAMIC VINEGAR

2 TABLESPOONS BABY CAPERS, CHOPPED

6 CORNICHONS (90G), CHOPPED

¼ CUP FINELY CHOPPED FRESH DILL

1 Preheat oven to 200°C/400°F.

2 Place sweet potato and oregano on a large oven tray. Drizzle with 1 tablespoon oil, season with salt; toss to coat. Roast for 30 minutes or until golden and tender.

3 Meanwhile, make yoghurt tartare.

4 Wrap fish in vine leaves; drizzle with remaining oil. Heat a large non-stick frying pan over medium heat. Cook fish, in batches, for 3 minutes on each side or until cooked through.

5 Serve fish with sweet potato chips, yoghurt tartare and lemon wedges. Top with dill.

YOGHURT TARTARE Combine ingredients in a medium bowl; season to taste.

za'atar snapper with burghul salad

SERVES 4

Spices and herbs are integral to a Mediterranean diet, adding flavour to dishes without fat or sugar. Some of the most common spices found in Mediterranean cuisine include cumin, saffron, sumac and za'atar. Common herbs of the region, used both in their fresh and dried forms, include oregano, sage, coriander, parsley, thyme, basil and rosemary.

TIP Salmon, blue-eye trevalla or barramundi can be used instead of snapper, if you like.

PREP + COOK TIME 30 MINUTES (+ STANDING)

1 TABLESPOON OLIVE OIL

1½ TABLESPOONS ZA'ATAR

4 X 180G (5½-OUNCE) BONELESS SNAPPER FILLETS

BURGHUL SALAD

1 MEDIUM RED ONION (170G), SLICED THINLY

1 CUP FRESH FLAT-LEAF PARSLEY

1 TABLESPOON FRESH THYME LEAVES

4 MEDIUM ROMA (EGG) TOMATOES (450G),
    CHOPPED COARSELY

100G (6½ OUNCES) RADISHES, SLICED THINLY

60G (2 OUNCES) BABY ROCKET (ARUGULA) LEAVES

¼ CUP (40G) FINE BURGHUL

1 TEASPOON GROUND SUMAC

2 TABLESPOONS LEMON JUICE

¼ CUP (60ML) EXTRA VIRGIN OLIVE OIL

1 Make burghul salad.

2 Combine oil, za'atar and fish in a large bowl; season. Cook fish in a heavy-based non-stick frying pan over medium-high heat for 2 minutes on each side or until browned and cooked through.

3 Serve fish with burghul salad.

BURGHUL SALAD Combine ingredients in a large bowl; season to taste. Stand for 15 minutes or until burghul is softened.

Family
Feasts

pumpkin & goat's cheese lasagne with rocket & pepita salad

SERVES 10

TIP You will need 3 medium pumpkins. To make it easier to halve the pumpkins, cut the stem end off each one first.

DO-AHEAD Lasagne can be prepared to the end of step 6 a day ahead; cover, refrigerate until required. Reheat in the oven.

PREP + COOK TIME 3 HOURS

3.4KG (12¾ POUNDS) BUTTERNUT PUMPKINS, HALVED LENGTHWAYS (SEE TIP)

2 TABLESPOONS EXTRA VIRGIN OLIVE OIL

4 MEDIUM LEEKS (1.4KG), SLICED THINLY

4 CLOVES GARLIC, CRUSHED

½ TEASPOON GROUND NUTMEG

1KG (2 POUNDS) FIRM RICOTTA

3 EGG YOLKS

1 TEASPOON FINELY GRATED LEMON RIND

1¼ CUPS (100G) FINELY GRATED PARMESAN

1 CUP (250ML) POURING CREAM

¼ CUP FINELY CHOPPED FRESH SAGE LEAVES

1½ TABLESPOONS FINELY CHOPPED FRESH CHIVES

6½ FRESH LASAGNE SHEETS

150G (4½ OUNCES) SOFT GOAT'S CHEESE, CRUMBLED

ROCKET & PEPITA SALAD

2 TEASPOONS LEMON JUICE

1 TEASPOON WHOLEGRAIN MUSTARD

1½ TABLESPOONS EXTRA VIRGIN OLIVE OIL

100G (3 OUNCES) BABY ROCKET (ARUGULA) LEAVES

¼ CUP PEPITAS (PUMPKIN SEED KERNELS), TOASTED

1 Preheat oven to 200°C/400°F.

2 Divide pumpkin halves, skin-side up, between two large oven trays; drizzle each pumpkin half with 1 tablespoon oil. Season. Cover with foil; bake for 2 hours or until very tender. Cool. Remove seeds, then peel away skin. Working in batches, place pumpkin in a large sieve over a bowl; leave to drain excess liquid, reserve. Transfer pumpkin to a bowl; mash with a potato masher.

3 Heat remaining oil in a large saucepan over medium heat; cook leek and garlic, stirring occasionally, for 10 minutes or until soft. Combine leek mixture, mashed pumpkin, nutmeg and reserved pumpkin liquid. Season to taste.

4 Process ricotta, egg yolks and rind, in batches until smooth. Add 1 cup (80g) of parmesan and the cream, pulse until just combined. Stir in herbs. Season.

5 Oil an ovenproof dish, around 24cm x 30cm x 6cm (9½-inch x 12-inch x 2½-inch) and 3.5 litres (14 cups) capacity. Place 2 lasagne sheets in base of dish. Spoon over a third of the ricotta mixture; smooth the surface. Top with half pumpkin mixture. Repeat layers, then top with 2½ lasagne sheets and another third of ricotta mixture. Sprinkle with goat's cheese and remaining parmesan. Cover with a layer of baking paper, then foil. (The lasagne will have three layers of pasta, two layers of pumpkin and three layers of ricotta mixture.)

6 Bake lasagne for 50 minutes. Remove foil and paper; bake for a further 15 minutes or until golden and hot. Stand 10 minutes.

7 Meanwhile, make rocket and pepita salad.

8 Serve lasagne with salad.

ROCKET & PEPITA SALAD Combine juice, mustard and oil in a large bowl; season to taste. Add rocket and pepitas; toss gently to combine.

Dips

While these favourite dips are readily available from the refrigerated section of most supermarkets and gourmet food stores, there is nothing better than making your own. Serve on platters with generous amounts of crackers, lavosh or vegetable sticks.

tzatziki

PREP TIME 15 MINUTES (+ REFRIGERATION) MAKES 1¼ CUPS

Place a fine sieve over a bowl, spoon in 500g (1lb) Greek-style yoghurt and ½ teaspoon salt. Cover, refrigerate for 2 hours or until thickened; discard liquid. Meanwhile, combine 1 coarsely grated lebanese cucumber and ½ teaspoon salt in a small bowl; stand for 20 minutes. Squeeze out excess liquid from cucumber. Combine yoghurt, cucumber, 1 clove crushed garlic and 2 tablespoons chopped fresh mint leaves; season to taste.

butter bean hummus

PREP + COOK TIME 10 MINUTES
MAKES 3 CUPS

Drain and rinse 800g (1½lbs) canned butter beans. Blend or process beans with ½ cup warm water, ¼ cup tahini, ¼ cup Greek-style yoghurt, 2 tablespoons lemon juice, 2 cloves crushed garlic and 3 teaspoons ground cumin until smooth; season to taste. Sprinkle with ground cumin to serve.

taramasalata

PREP + COOK TIME 25 MINUTES
(+ REFRIGERATION) MAKES 1⅔ CUPS

Boil, steam or microwave 1 coarsely chopped large potato until tender; cool. Refrigerate until cold. Mash potato in a small bowl with 90g (3oz) tarama (salted fish roe), ½ finely grated small white onion, ¾ cup extra virgin olive oil, ¼ cup white wine vinegar and 1 tablespoon lemon juice until smooth. Season with pepper; serve drizzled with extra oil.

greek roast lamb leg with lemon potatoes & skordalia

SERVES 4

Skordalia is a classic Greek accompaniment to meat, made from either potato or bread pureed with garlic, olive oil, lemon juice or vinegar, herbs and, occasionally, ground nuts.

TIP Sprinkle roast lamb with extra fresh lemon thyme sprigs, if you like.

PREP + COOK TIME 4 HOURS 45 MINUTES (+ REFRIGERATION)

2 CLOVES GARLIC, CRUSHED

½ CUP (125ML) LEMON JUICE

2 TABLESPOONS EXTRA VIRGIN OLIVE OIL

1 TABLESPOON FRESH OREGANO LEAVES

1 TEASPOON FRESH LEMON THYME LEAVES

2KG (4-POUND) LAMB LEG

LEMON WEDGES, TO SERVE

SKORDALIA

1 MEDIUM POTATO (200G), QUARTERED

3 CLOVES GARLIC, QUARTERED

1 TABLESPOON LEMON JUICE

1 TABLESPOON WHITE WINE VINEGAR

2 TABLESPOONS WATER

⅓ CUP (80ML) EXTRA VIRGIN OLIVE OIL

1 TABLESPOON WARM WATER

LEMON POTATOES

5 LARGE POTATOES (1.5KG), QUARTERED

1 MEDIUM LEMON (140G), RIND PEELED INTO
  6 WIDE STRIPS

2 TABLESPOONS LEMON JUICE

2 TABLESPOONS EXTRA VIRGIN OLIVE OIL

1 Combine garlic, juice, oil, oregano and thyme leaves in a large non-reactive bowl; add lamb, turn to coat in mixture. Cover; refrigerate for 3 hours or overnight.

2 Preheat oven to 160°C/325°F.

3 Place marinated lamb in a large roasting pan; roast for 3½ hours.

4 Meanwhile, make skordalia, then lemon potatoes.

5 Add lemon potatoes to oven; roast alongside lamb for the last 30 minutes of lamb cooking time.

6 Remove lamb from oven; stand, covered loosely with foil.

7 Increase oven to 220°C/425°F; roast potatoes a further 20 minutes or until golden.

8 Serve roast lamb with lemon potatoes, skordalia and lemon wedges.

SKORDALIA Boil, steam or microwave potato until tender; drain. Push potato through a ricer or fine sieve into a medium bowl; cool 10 minutes. Add garlic, juice, vinegar and the water to potato; stir until well combined. Place potato mixture in blender; with motor operating, gradually add oil in a thin, steady stream, blending only until skordalia thickens (do not over-mix or the sauce will become gluey). Stir in the warm water.

LEMON POTATOES Combine potato, rind, juice and oil in a large bowl; season. Place, in a single layer, on an oven tray.

barbecued octopus

SERVES 4

Octopus is usually tenderised before you buy them. Like squid, octopus requires either long slow cooking (usually for larger molluscs) or quick cooking over high heat (usually for small molluscs) – anything in between will make them tough and rubbery. When barbecuing, make sure the grill plate or barbecue is very hot before adding the baby octopus.

TIPS Ask your fishmonger to clean the octopus for you. Preheat the grill plate for at least 10 minutes before cooking for really fast, high-heat cooking. If you have nasturtium leaves, sprinkle these over the salad as well, if you like.

PREP + COOK TIME 30 MINUTES (+ REFRIGERATION)

3 MEDIUM LEMONS (420G)

⅓ CUP (80ML) EXTRA VIRGIN OLIVE OIL

½ TEASPOON DRIED OREGANO LEAVES

2 CLOVES GARLIC, CRUSHED

1KG (1 POUND) BABY OCTOPUS, CLEANED (SEE TIPS)

4 FRESH LONG RED CHILLIES

ROCKET (ARUGULA) LEAVES AND FRESH FLAT-LEAF
    PARSLEY LEAVES, TO SERVE

1 Finely grated rind from 1 lemon; squeeze juice. Place rind, juice, oil, oregano and garlic in a screw-top jar; shake well. Season to taste.

2 Place octopus and half the dressing in a large bowl; toss to coat in mixture. Cover; refrigerate for 30 minutes.

3 Cook octopus on a heated grill plate (or pan or barbecue) over high heat for 6 minutes or until browned and tender. Cover loosely with foil.

4 Cut remaining lemons in half crossways; cook, cut-side down, on heated grill plate (or pan or barbecue) for 2 minutes or until browned. Transfer to a plate. Cook whole chillies for 4 minutes or until slightly blackened; slice thickly.

5 Combine octopus with remaining dressing, chilli and leaves; serve with char-grilled lemons.

fisherman's soup with turmeric rouille

SERVES 4

Bouillabaisse, by any other name, was created by the fishermen of Marseille from the items of the daily catch that weren't sold to restaurants. The recipe varies, depending on what fish and shellfish are available. It's served topped with rouille – a garlicky mayonnaise with saffron. We've used fresh turmeric in our rouille for a similar colour and added nutiritional benefits.

TIPS For details on how to clean calamari, see Glossary, page 235. You could also use squid hoods, if preferred. Use a tiny pinch of saffron powder instead of threads, if you like. If fresh turmeric is unavailable, use a pinch of saffron threads or powder in the rouille instead.

PREP + COOK TIME 1 HOUR

8 UNCOOKED LARGE KING PRAWNS (SHRIMP) (560G)

2 BLUE SWIMMER CRABS (860G)

2 MEDIUM CALAMARI (320G), CLEANED, TENTACLES RESERVED (SEE TIPS)

300G (9½ OUNCES) SKINLESS BONELESS FIRM WHITE FISH FILLETS

1 TABLESPOON EXTRA VIRGIN OLIVE OIL

1 MEDIUM ONION (150G), SLICED THICKLY

2 CLOVES GARLIC, SLICED THINLY

2 BABY FENNEL BULBS (260G), TRIMMED, SLICED THINLY, FRONDS RESERVED

1 FRESH LONG RED CHILLI, SLICED THINLY

PINCH SAFFRON THREADS

1 BAY LEAF

2 CUPS (500ML) VEGETABLE STOCK

2 CUPS (500ML) WATER

400G (12½ OUNCES) CANNED CHERRY TOMATOES

TURMERIC ROUILLE

2 EGG YOLKS

1 CLOVE GARLIC, CHOPPED COARSELY

2 TEASPOONS WHITE BALSAMIC VINEGAR

1 TEASPOON DIJON MUSTARD

½ TEASPOON FINELY GRATED FRESH TURMERIC (SEE TIPS)

1 CUP (250ML) EXTRA VIRGIN OLIVE OIL

1 Peel and devein prawns, leaving tails intact. Quarter crabs; clean. Slice calamari. Cut fish into 4cm (1½-inch) pieces.

2 Heat oil in large saucepan over medium-high heat; cook onion, garlic and fennel, stirring, for 5 minutes or until soft. Add chilli, saffron and bay leaf; cook, stirring, for 2 minutes or until fragrant. Add stock, the water and tomatoes; bring to the boil. Reduce heat to low; cook, covered, for 30 minutes.

3 Meanwhile, make turmeric rouille.

4 Add prawns, crab, calamari and fish to pan; cook, covered, for 8 minutes or until seafood is just cooked.

5 Serve soup topped with rouille and reserved fennel fronds.

TURMERIC ROUILLE Process yolks, garlic, vinegar, mustard and turmeric in a small food processor until smooth. With motor operating, gradually add oil in a thin stream until mixture is thick. Season to taste.

spanish fish skewers with smoky romesco sauce

SERVES 4

Romesco is a traditional northern Spanish sauce, much like pesto in texture, made from a mixture of nuts and fire-roasted capsicum that often accompanies fish and seafood. Romesco also goes well with barbecued meats or char-grilled vegetables such as eggplant and zucchini.

TIPS You will need 12 bamboo or metal skewers for this recipe. Soak the bamboo skewers for 10 minutes in boiling water before using to prevent them burning during cooking; oil metal skewers to prevent sticking. We used blue-eye trevalla but you could use snapper, ling or barramundi.

DO-AHEAD Romesco can be made a day ahead; keep covered in the fridge.

PREP + COOK TIME 1 HOUR 45 MINUTES (+ COOLING & REFRIGERATION)

2 SMALL RED CAPSICUMS (BELL PEPPERS) (300G), QUARTERED

3 CLOVES GARLIC, UNPEELED

750G (1½ POUNDS) SKINLESS BONELESS FIRM WHITE FISH FILLETS, CUT INTO 2.5CM (1-INCH) PIECES

2 TEASPOONS SMOKED PAPRIKA

⅓ CUP (80ML) EXTRA VIRGIN OLIVE OIL

2 TEASPOONS FINELY GRATED LEMON RIND

2 TABLESPOONS FINELY CHOPPED FRESH FLAT-LEAF PARSLEY LEAVES

24 FRESH BAY LEAVES

¼ CUP (40G) BLANCHED ALMONDS

2 TABLESPOONS LEMON JUICE

2 MEDIUM LEMONS (280G), HALVED

1 Preheat grill (broiler) on high heat. Place capsicum, skin-side up, and garlic on an oven tray. Cook under grill for 15 minutes or until skins are blackened. Transfer to a medium bowl. Cover with plastic wrap; cool.

2 Combine fish with half the paprika, half the oil, the rind and parsley in a medium bowl; season. Thread fish and bay leaves onto 12 skewers. Place on a tray; cover, refrigerate.

3 Meanwhile, remove and discard skins from capsicum and garlic. Process capsicum, garlic, almonds, juice, remaining paprika and remaining oil until almost smooth. Transfer romesco to a small bowl; season to taste.

4 Cook fish skewers a large heavy-based frying pan over medium-high heat for 4 minutes or until browned all over and cooked through. Add lemon halves to pan; cook for 1 minute or until browned.

5 Serve fish skewers with romesco sauce and cooked lemon halves.

baked salmon with tabbouleh & tahini sauce

SERVES 4

Sumac adds a tart, lemony flavour to dishes making it a perfect pairing with fish. The Romans used this ground spice as a sour element in cooking before lemons were introduced to their culinary world. It also goes well with chicken and meat, sprinkled on vegetables or in a salad dressing – any foods you would ordinarily match with a fresh citrus flavour.

TIPS Burghul (cracked wheat) can be bought from health food stores. Use regular cherry or grape tomatoes, if preferred.

DO-AHEAD
You can make the tabbouleh and tahini sauce several hours ahead; refrigerate, covered, until ready to use.

PREP + COOK TIME 50 MINUTES

700G (1½ POUND) PIECE SKINLESS BONELESS
SALMON FILLET

1½ TEASPOONS SUMAC

2 TABLESPOONS EXTRA VIRGIN OLIVE OIL

LEMON WEDGES, TO SERVE

TABBOULEH

1 CUP SMALL FRESH FLAT-LEAF PARSLEY LEAVES

¼ CUP SMALL FRESH MINT LEAVES

2 GREEN ONIONS (SCALLIONS), SLICED THINLY

½ CUP (80G) COARSE BURGHUL (SEE TIPS)

1½ CUPS (375ML) WATER

200G (6½ OUNCES) BABY HEIRLOOM TOMATOES,
QUARTERED (SEE TIPS)

1 TABLESPOON LEMON JUICE

TAHINI SAUCE

½ CUP (140G) GREEK-STYLE YOGHURT

1½ TABLESPOONS TAHINI

1 CLOVE GARLIC, CRUSHED

2 TEASPOONS LEMON JUICE

1 Make tabbouleh, then tahini sauce.

2 Preheat oven to 200°C/400°F.

3 Line an oven tray with baking paper. Place salmon on tray; sprinkle with 1 teaspoon of the sumac, then drizzle with the oil. Season. Bake for 20 minutes or until salmon is almost cooked through.

4 Top baked salmon with reserved herb mixture and remaining sumac; serve with tabbouleh, tahini sauce, and lemon wedges.

TABBOULEH Combine herbs and green onion in a large bowl; reserve half the mixture for serving. Bring burghul and the water to the boil in a small saucepan; reduce heat to low. Cook for 20 minutes or until tender; drain. Transfer burghul to a large bowl; add tomato and lemon juice. Toss gently to combine; season to taste.

TAHINI SAUCE Whisk ingredients in a small bowl until combined; season to taste.

lamb, spinach & fetta pie

SERVES 6

The filling for this pie is quintessentially Greek with its thick and flavoursome tomato-based lamb sauce with spinach leaves and fetta. For individual pies, spoon filling mixture into six 1-cup (250ml) ovenproof dishes. Cut the pastry into smaller rectangles; place slightly overlapping to cover the filling. Keep an eye on the pastry while baking as the cooking time will differ from the large pie.

TIP The spinach can be replaced with silver beet or even kale if you prefer; simply discard the tough centre stalks first.

PREP + COOK TIME 1 HOUR 20 MINUTES (+ STANDING)

¼ CUP (60ML) EXTRA VIRGIN OLIVE OIL

2 MEDIUM ONIONS (300G), CHOPPED FINELY

3 TRIMMED CELERY STALKS (450G), CHOPPED FINELY

4 CLOVES GARLIC, CRUSHED

1KG (2 POUNDS) MINCED (GROUND) LAMB

½ CUP (125ML) DRY RED WINE

1½ CUPS (375ML) VEGETABLE STOCK

800G (1½ POUNDS) CANNED CRUSHED TOMATOES

⅓ CUP (95G) TOMATO PASTE

1 TABLESPOON FRESH CHOPPED OREGANO LEAVES

2 CINNAMON STICKS

150G (4½ OUNCES) GREEK FETTA, CRUMBLED

100G (3 OUNCES) BABY SPINACH LEAVES

2 SHEETS SHORTCRUST PASTRY

1 EGG

1 EGG YOLK

1 TEASPOON SEA SALT FLAKES

1 TEASPOON FENNEL SEEDS

1 Preheat oven to 220°C/425°F.

2 Heat oil in a large frying pan over medium heat; cook onion and celery, stirring, for 5 minutes or until browned lightly. Add garlic; cook for 1 minute.

3 Increase heat to high, add lamb; cook, stirring, until browned, breaking it up with the back of a wooden spoon. Add wine; cook for 2 minutes. Add stock, tomatoes, paste, oregano and cinnamon; cook for 35 minutes or until the liquid is evaporated and sauce is thick. Cool.

4 Stir fetta and spinach into lamb mixture, season to taste; spoon into a 20cm (8-inch) round pie tin or 1.5-litre (6-cup) ovenproof dish.

5 Cut each sheet of pastry into ten equal rectangles. Place pastry rectangles, slightly overlapping to cover filling. Brush pastry with combined beaten egg and egg yolk; sprinkle with salt and fennel seeds.

6 Bake pie for 25 minutes or until pastry is a deep golden; cover the pastry with pieces of foil if it starts to overbrown. Stand for 10 minutes before serving.

Shared Plates

Tapas, mezze or antipasto – it all means the same thing. Lots of bowls and platters filled with bite-sized or individual foods on the table for the family to help themselves. Serve with torn pieces of bread and plenty of wine.

stuffed zucchini flowers

PREP + COOK TIME 25 MINUTES   MAKES 18

Combine 250g (8oz) firm ricotta, 50g (1½oz) finely chopped greek fetta, 2 tablespoons finely chopped fresh mint leaves, 2 teaspoons finely grated lemon rind, ½ teaspoon dried chilli flakes, 1 clove crushed garlic and 1 egg yolk in a medium bowl; season to taste. Carefully open 18 zucchini flowers then remove the yellow stamens from inside the flowers. Spoon ricotta mixture into flowers, leaving a 1cm (½in) gap at the top. Twist petal tops to enclose the filling. Heat 2 tablespoons extra virgin olive oil in a non-stick frying pan over high heat; cook flowers for 1 minute on each side or until light golden and heated through; season to taste. Sprinkle with finely grated lemon rind and mint leaves.

baked fetta
with roasted garlic,
chilli & olives

PREP + COOK TIME 1 HOUR 25 MINUTES SERVES 10

Preheat oven to 180°C/350°F. Place 10 peeled
cloves of garlic and ¼ cup extra virgin olive oil in a
small ovenproof dish (ensure garlic is completely
covered by oil). Cover with foil; bake for 30 minutes
or until tender. Cool slightly. Increase oven to
200°C/400°F. Pat 700g (1lbs) greek fetta dry
with paper towel. Cut into 4cm (1½in) thick slices;
place in an ovenproof dish, just large enough for
fetta to fit in a single layer. Pour ¼ cup additional
extra virgin olive oil and the garlic in oil over fetta;
top with 2 sprigs fresh rosemary, 3 teaspoons fresh
oregano leaves, ⅓ cup ligurian olives and ½ thinly
sliced fresh long red chilli. Bake for 40 minutes or
until fetta is soft and lightly browned. Serve with
toasted or grilled pitta bread.

dukkah prawn
skewers

PREP + COOK TIME 15 MINUTES SERVES 4

Shell and devein 1.2kg (2½lbs) uncooked
large king prawns (shrimp), leaving tails
intact. Combine ¼ cup pistachio dukkah,
2 tablespoons extra virgin olive oil, 2 cloves
crushed garlic and 2 teaspoons finely
grated lemon rind in a large bowl; add
prawns, toss to coat in mixture. Thread
prawns onto 8 bamboo or metal skewers.
Heat a heavy-based frying pan over high
heat; cook skewers, turning, until prawns
change colour. Serve with lemon wedges.

salt-crusted whole fish with celeriac remoulade

SERVES 4

Cooking food in a salt crust helps retain the juices and enhances the flavour. It's important to press the dampened salt mixture firmly all over the fish so that none of it is exposed directly to the heat of the oven. After cooking, the crust should be very hard and browned. Use a hammer or meat mallet and an old knife to break open the crust; the scales and skin should lift off with the crust.

TIPS The salt crust keeps the fish moist and lightly seasons the flesh during cooking. To fillet the fish for serving, make a diagonal cut near the gills and tails, then down the middle of the back along the spine. Lift the top fillet off with a spatula. Peel away the bones and remove base fillet. Remove any salt mixture clinging to the fish.

DO-AHEAD Celeriac remoulade can be made a day ahead; store covered in the fridge.

PREP + COOK TIME 45 MINUTES (+ STANDING)

1KG (2 POUNDS) WHOLE SNAPPER OR
    SILVER PERCH, CLEANED

1 MEDIUM LEMON (140G), SLICED

2 FRESH DILL SPRIGS

5 CUPS (1.35KG) COARSE COOKING SALT

3 EGG WHITES

LEMON WEDGES, TO SERVE

CELERIAC REMOULADE

1 SMALL CELERIAC (500G)

⅓ CUP (100G) WHOLE-EGG MAYONNAISE

2 TABLESPOONS THINLY SLICED CORNICHONS

1 TABLESPOON LEMON JUICE

1 TABLESPOON DIJON MUSTARD

1 TABLESPOON BABY CAPERS

1 Preheat oven to 200°C/400°F. Line a large oven tray with foil.

2 Use kitchen scissors to snip off fish fins and trim tail. Place lemon slices and dill sprigs in fish cavity.

3 Combine salt and egg whites in a large bowl until the consistency feels like sand. Spread one-third of the salt mixture on the tray. Place fish on top of salt; cover fish completely with remaining salt mixture, moulding it tightly around the fish to seal.

4 Bake fish for 25 minutes. To check the fish is cooked, insert a sharp knife through the crust into the thickest part of the fish; wait 5 seconds. Slowly withdraw knife and touch the flat side of the blade to the inside of your wrist. If the blade is hot, the fish is cooked. Stand for 10 minutes.

5 Meanwhile, make celeriac remoulade.

6 Break crust around edges of fish and gently lift the crust off. Remove and discard fish skin. Serve fish with remoulade and lemon wedges.

CELERIAC REMOULADE Peel celeriac; cut into matchsticks. Place celeriac in a medium heatproof bowl with enough boiling water to cover; stand for 30 seconds, drain. Refresh in another bowl of iced water; drain. Return celeriac to bowl with remaining ingredients; mix well. Season to taste.

almond gremolata roast chicken

SERVES 4

Gremolata is a versatile condiment and garnish – sprinkled on a dish just before serving, the scent of the combined ingredients once they hit the heat excites the palate. Originally based on garlic, lemon rind and parsley, there are many variations using other citrus rinds such as orange, or adding pine nuts and finely grated parmesan. We've added roasted almonds for flavour and crunch.

TIP Swap orange rind for lemon rind in the chicken coating and gremolata, if you like.

PREP + COOK TIME 2 HOURS

½ CUP (80G) ROASTED ALMONDS, CHOPPED

4 FRESH SAGE LEAVES

1 TEASPOON FINELY GRATED LEMON RIND (SEE TIP)

2 CLOVES GARLIC, CHOPPED COARSELY

⅓ CUP (80ML) EXTRA VIRGIN OLIVE OIL

1.8KG (3½-POUND) WHOLE CHICKEN

¼ BUNCH CELERY (375G), PALE INNER LEAVES
   RESERVED

¼ LOAF (150G) SOURDOUGH BREAD, TORN INTO
   4CM (1½ INCH) PIECES

2 BABY PARSNIPS (240G), CUT INTO EIGHTHS

2 BUNCHES (800G) RAINBOW BABY (DUTCH)
   CARROTS, TRIMMED, HALVED LENGTHWAYS

1 CUPS (250ML) CHICKEN STOCK

ALMOND GREMOLATA

½ CUP (80G) FINELY CHOPPED ROASTED ALMONDS

1 SMALL CLOVE GARLIC, CRUSHED

3 TEASPOONS FINELY GRATED LEMON RIND (SEE TIP)

⅓ CUP FINELY CHOPPED FRESH FLAT-LEAF
   PARSLEY LEAVES

1 Preheat oven to 200°C/400°F. Oil a large roasting pan.

2 Blend or process almonds, sage, rind, garlic and 1½ tablespoons oil until a rough paste forms; season.

3 Pat chicken dry with paper towel. Spread almond mixture evenly between chicken skin and breast and tops of the legs. Place chicken in oiled pan; season.

4 Place celery around chicken; top with bread. Drizzle with another 1½ tablespoons of the oil.

5 Place parsnip, carrot and stock in another large roasting pan; drizzle with remaining oil. Season. Roast chicken and vegetables for 1¼ hours or until chicken is cooked through. Transfer chicken, breast-side down, to a tray; cover loosely with foil. Stand for 15 minutes. Roast vegetables for a further 20 minutes or until golden and tender.

6 Make almond gremolata.

7 Serve chicken with sourdough and vegetables, sprinkled with almond gremolata.

ALMOND GREMOLATA Combine ingredients in a small bowl; season to taste.

beetroot, haloumi, chickpea & rice winter salad

SERVES 4

Canned chickpeas must be drained of their liquid before using. Empty the contents of the can into a strainer, allowing the liquid to drain away. Hold the strainer under cold running water and rinse the chickpeas well. The chickpea liquid, called aquafaba, can be reserved and whipped into peaks like you would egg white, for a vegan-friendly meringue, pavlova or mousse.

TIP You can replace the haloumi with crumbled goat's cheese or fetta, if you like.

PREP + COOK TIME 30 MINUTES

1 CUP (200G) BROWN RICE

⅓ CUP (80ML) EXTRA VIRGIN OLIVE OIL

1 SMALL RED ONION (100G), CUT INTO WEDGES

1 TEASPOON GROUND CUMIN

1 TEASPOON GROUND CORIANDER

400G (12½ OUNCES) CANNED CHICKPEAS
(GARBANZO BEANS), DRAINED, RINSED

500G (1 POUND) PACKAGED PRE-COOKED
BEETROOT (BEETS), QUARTERED

100G (3 OUNCES) BABY SPINACH LEAVES

1 CUP LOOSELY PACKED FRESH MINT LEAVES

½ CUP (50G) WALNUTS, ROASTED,
CHOPPED COARSELY

2 TABLESPOONS BALSAMIC GLAZE

200G (6½ OUNCES) HALOUMI, SLICED

1 Cook rice in a large saucepan of boiling water for 25 minutes or until just tender; drain.

2 Meanwhile, heat 1 tablespoon of oil in a large frying pan over medium heat. Add onion; cook, stirring, for 5 minutes or until tender. Add cumin and coriander; cook, stirring, for 30 seconds or until fragrant. Add chickpeas and beetroot; stir until heated through.

3 Meanwhile, combine rice, spinach, mint and walnuts in a large bowl. Drizzle with combined 1 tablespoon balsamic glaze and 2 tablespoons oil. Add beetroot and chickpea mixture; toss gently. Season.

4 Heat remaining oil in a large frying pan over high heat. Cook haloumi for 2 minutes on each side or until golden.

5 Serve salad with haloumi, drizzled with remaining balsamic glaze.

eggplant parmigiana

SERVES 4

With its national colours of red, white and green, this layered dish is pure Italian comfort food. Eggplant is sliced and shallow-fried until golden on both sides and soft on the inside. In an ovenproof dish, layer the cooked eggplant slices with a rich tomato sauce, then top with sliced bocconcini. Bake until the eggplant becomes melt-in-your-mouth tender. Sprinkle with basil before serving.

SERVING SUGGESTIONS
Serve with a rocket (arugula) salad and crusty bread or stir through cooked short pasta.

PREP + COOK TIME 1 HOUR 15 MINUTES

⅔ CUP (160ML) EXTRA VIRGIN OLIVE OIL

1 MEDIUM ONION (150G), CHOPPED FINELY

2 CLOVES GARLIC, CRUSHED

400G (12½ OUNCES) CANNED CRUSHED TOMATOES

2 CUPS (560G) BOTTLED TOMATO PASSATA

¼ TEASPOON DRIED CHILLI FLAKES

2 MEDIUM EGGPLANTS (600G), SLICED THICKLY

¼ CUP (35G) PLAIN (ALL-PURPOSE) FLOUR

⅓ CUP FRESH BASIL LEAVES

200G (6½ OUNCES) BOCCONCINI, SLICED THINLY

⅔ CUP (50G) FINELY GRATED PARMESAN

½ TEASPOON SWEET PAPRIKA

SMALL BASIL LEAVES, EXTRA, TO SERVE

1 Preheat oven to 180°C/350°F.

2 Heat 1 tablespoon oil in a large frying pan over medium heat; cook onion, stirring, until soft. Add garlic; cook, stirring, until fragrant. Stir in tomatoes, passata and chilli; season to taste. Transfer mixture to a medium jug.

3 Toss eggplant in flour to coat; shake off excess. Heat remaining oil in same cleaned pan; cook eggplant, in batches, until browned on both sides. Drain on paper towel.

4 Layer half the eggplant in a 26cm (10½-inch) round, 5cm (2-inch) deep ovenproof dish; season. Top with half the tomato mixture, basil and bocconcini. Repeat layering, finishing with parmesan; sprinkle with paprika.

5 Bake, covered, for 30 minutes. Uncover, bake for a further 15 minutes or until browned and tender. Serve topped with extra basil.

cheese & silver beet borek with crunchy seeds

SERVES 6

Silver beet, sometimes mistakenly called spinach in greengrocers (and true spinach can be mislabeled english spinach), is also called swiss chard to further confuse the issue. One thing for certain, however, is that it should be used in this recipe rather than spinach, for its stronger flavour, hardier texture and because its leaves contain far less water than spinach, the pastry is more likely to stay crisp.

TIP Use cottage cheese instead of ricotta, if preferred.

PREP + COOK TIME 1 HOUR 20 MINUTES

6 LARGE STALKS SILVER BEET (SWISS CHARD) (480G)

5 EGGS

500G (1 POUND) FIRM RICOTTA CHEESE (SEE TIP)

200G (6½ OUNCES) GREEK FETTA, CRUMBLED

1 CUP (240G) SOUR CREAM

¾ CUP (180ML) SODA WATER

290G (9½ OUNCES) FILLO PASTRY

OLIVE-OIL SPRAY

1 TEASPOON POPPY SEEDS

1 TABLESPOON SUNFLOWER SEED KERNELS

1 TABLESPOON PEPITAS (PUMPKIN SEED KERNELS)

GREEK-STYLE YOGHURT, TO SERVE

1 MEDIUM LEMON (140G), CUT INTO WEDGES

1 Preheat oven to 170°C/325°F. Oil and line a 22cm x 32cm x 6cm (8¾-inch x 12¾-inch x 2½-inch) ovenproof dish with baking paper, extending the paper 2cm (¾ inch) over sides.

2 Trim 4cm (1½ inches) from silver beet stems; separate leaves and stems. Finely shred leaves; finely chop stems. You will need 4 cups shredded leaves and 1½ cups finely chopped stems.

3 Heat a lightly oiled large frying pan over high heat; cook silver beet leaves and stems for 2 minutes or until wilted and tender. When cool enough to handle, squeeze liquid from silver beet; set aside to cool.

4 Whisk 4 of the eggs in a large bowl until combined. Add ricotta, fetta, sour cream, soda water and silver beet, stir to combine; season.

5 Layer five sheets of pastry, spraying each sheet with oil; place on base of dish, trimming to fit. Keep remaining sheets covered with baking paper topped with a clean, damp tea towel to prevent them from drying out. Pour 1 cup of cheese mixture onto pastry.

6 Layer two sheets of pastry, spraying each sheet with oil; place on cheese mixture. Pour 1 cup of cheese mixture on pastry. Repeat layering with two more layers of pastry and remaining cheese mixture. Layer five sheets of pastry, spraying each sheet with oil; place on cheese mixture.

7 Whisk remaining egg lightly; brush over top of pie. Sprinkle pie with combined seeds; bake for 40 minutes or until golden and cooked through.

8 Serve pie with yoghurt and lemon wedges.

green barley salad

SERVES 6

When in season, buy fresh broad beans in the pod for this recipe (see tips); you will need to remove the outer shell. Leave the grey skins intact for now as the recipe will direct you when to remove them. Once the broad beans are blanched, pop the bright green beans from their leathery grey overcoats while they are still warm. Blanching peas and beans briefly, helps to retain their bright spring colour.

TIPS If fresh broad beans in the pod are available, use 500g (1 pound) of these instead to yield 1 cup podded beans. Swap your favourite fetta for labne, if you like.

PREP + COOK TIME 30 MINUTES

1 CUP (200G) PEARL BARLEY

3 CUPS (750ML) WATER

1 CUP (120G) FROZEN PEAS

1 CUP (150G) FROZEN BROAD (FAVA) BEANS (SEE TIPS)

150G (4½ OUNCES) GREEN BEANS, TRIMMED, HALVED LENGTHWAYS

1 LEBANESE CUCUMBER (130G), HALVED LENGTHWAYS, SLICED THINLY

1 BABY COS LETTUCE (180G), TRIMMED, TORN

2 GREEN ONIONS (SCALLIONS), SLICED THINLY

½ CUP FRESH MINT LEAVES

2 TABLESPOONS EXTRA VIRGIN OLIVE OIL

1 TABLESPOON LEMON JUICE

335G (10½ OUNCES) LABNE IN OLIVE OIL, DRAINED (SEE TIPS)

1 Place barley and the water in a medium saucepan, bring to the boil; reduce heat to low. Cook, covered, for 35 minutes or until tender. Drain; rinse under cold water until cool.

2 Meanwhile, cook peas, broad beans and green beans in a large saucepan of boiling water for 2 minutes or until just tender; drain. Refresh under cold running water; drain well. Remove grey skins from broad beans.

3 Transfer barley and pea mixture to a large bowl; add cucumber, lettuce, green onion and mint. Drizzle with combined oil and juice; toss gently to combine.

4 Top salad with labne and season to taste.

black rice seafood paella
SERVES 4

Short-grain rice varieties such as black rice are the most suitable for paella. It adds a lovely nutty taste and becomes almost purple in colour when cooked. The traditional pan for this Spanish recipe is shallow and wide. If you don't have a paella pan or heavy-based frying pan large enough, use two smaller frying pans as the mixture should only be about 4cm (1½ inches) deep.

TIPS Black rice is available from some supermarkets and Asian food stores. Recipe is best made just before serving.

PREP + COOK TIME 1 HOUR

8 UNCOOKED LARGE KING PRAWNS (SHRIMP) (560G)

¼ CUP (60ML) EXTRA VIRGIN OLIVE OIL

1 MEDIUM WHITE ONION (150G), CHOPPED FINELY

1½ TEASPOONS SMOKED PAPRIKA

1 SMALL RED CAPSICUM (BELL PEPPER) (150G), SLICED THICKLY

2 CLOVES GARLIC, CHOPPED

1 CUP (200G) BLACK RICE, RINSED

400G (12½ OUNCES) CANNED CHERRY TOMATOES

2 CUPS (500ML) VEGETABLE STOCK

2 CUPS (500ML) WATER

300G (9½ OUNCES) SKINLESS BONELESS FIRM WHITE FISH FILLETS, CUT INTO 4CM (1½-INCH) PIECES

4 SCALLOPS ON HALF SHELL (100G)

8 PIPIS (320G)

¼ CUP FRESH FLAT-LEAF PARSLEY LEAVES

LEMON WEDGES, TO SERVE

1 Shell and devein prawns, leaving tails intact.

2 Heat oil in a large heavy-based frying pan or paella pan over medium heat; cook onion, stirring, for 3 minutes or until softened. Add paprika, capsicum, garlic and rice; cook, stirring, for 2 minutes or until well combined. Add tomatoes, stock and the water; bring to the boil. Reduce heat to low; cook, stirring occasionally, for 40 minutes or until most of the liquid has been absorbed and rice is tender.

3 Arrange seafood on rice mixture; season. Cook, covered, for 5 minutes or until seafood is just cooked through.

4 Serve paella with parsley and lemon wedges.

provençale beef casserole
SERVES 4

If you wouldn't drink it, don't cook with it: that's the rule of thumb for choosing wine for cooking. Cheap, inferior quality wines will impart a less pleasant flavour than a great drinking wine. Serve a hearty casserole such as this with mashed potato or crusty bread to mop up the sauce.

SERVING
SUGGESTION
Serve with mashed
potato or toasted
sourdough bread,
if you like.

PREP + COOK TIME 1 HOURS 50 MINUTES

2 TABLESPOONS EXTRA VIRGIN OLIVE OIL

1KG (2 POUNDS) GRAVY BEEF, CUT INTO
2CM (¾-INCH) PIECES

2 RINDLESS BACON SLICES (130G),
CHOPPED COARSELY

1 MEDIUM LEEK (350G), SLICED THINLY

2 MEDIUM CARROTS (240G), DICED

1 STALK CELERY (150G), TRIMMED, DICED

2 CLOVES GARLIC, CRUSHED

400G (12½ OUNCES) CANNED CRUSHED TOMATOES

1½ CUPS (375ML) BEEF STOCK

1 CUP (250ML) DRY RED WINE

2 BAY LEAVES

4 SPRIGS FRESH THYME

6 SPRIGS FRESH FLAT-LEAF PARSLEY

2 MEDIUM ZUCCHINI (240G), SLICED

½ CUP (75G) PITTED BLACK OLIVES

1 Heat oil in large heavy-based saucepan; cook beef, in batches, until browned. Remove from pan.

2 Cook bacon, leek, carrot, celery and garlic in same pan, stirring, for 5 minutes or until leek softens.

3 Return beef to pan, add tomatoes, stock, wine, bay leaves, thyme and parsley; bring to the boil. Reduce heat to low; cook, covered, for 1 hour, stirring occasionally.

4 Add zucchini and olives; cook, covered, for 30 minutes or until beef is tender. Remove and discard thyme and parsley before serving.

lamb bretonne

SERVES 4

Hearty and comforting, this French-style lamb roast will become a Sunday favourite. The lamb leg is prepared in the same classic way, pierced all over, studded with garlic and rosemary then seasoned well. For the French twist from Brittany, add white beans, tomatoes and stock, before putting it in the oven for 2 hours. Serve with mashed potatoes and steamed green vegetables.

TIP Swap canned borlotti beans for cannellini beans, if you like.

PREP + COOK TIME 2 HOURS 30 MINUTES

1.5KG (3 POUND) LEG OF LAMB

1 CLOVE GARLIC, SLICED THINLY

2 SPRIGS FRESH ROSEMARY

1 TABLESPOON EXTRA VIRGIN OLIVE OIL

2 MEDIUM ONIONS (300G), SLICED THINLY

3 CLOVES GARLIC, CRUSHED

400G (12½ OUNCES) CANNED CRUSHED TOMATOES

410G (13 OUNCES) CANNED TOMATO PUREE

2 CUPS (500ML) BEEF STOCK

400G (12½ OUNCES) CANNED CANNELLINI BEANS, DRAINED, RINSED (SEE TIP)

1 Preheat oven to 180°C/350°F.

2 Trim excess fat from lamb. Pierce lamb in several places with a sharp knife; press sliced garlic and a little of the rosemary firmly into cuts. Season lamb.

3 Heat oil in a large flameproof roasting pan over medium heat; cook onion and crushed garlic, stirring, for 5 minutes or until onion browns slightly. Stir in tomatoes, puree, stock, beans and remaining rosemary; bring to the boil.

4 Place lamb, pierced-side down, on bean mixture, cover; transfer to oven. Cook for 1 hour. Uncover, turn lamb carefully; cook, brushing occasionally with tomato mixture, for 1 hour for medium or until lamb is cooked as desired.

baby octopus & eggplant in tomato & caper sauce

SERVES 6

While baby octopus is usually char-grilled or fast-fried, here we cook it Italian-style, stirring it in a saucepan with classic Mediterranean flavours. The secret is not to overcook it or its flesh will toughen. When purchasing fresh octopus, look for shiny intact skin and a pleasant smell of the sea.

TIP Octopus is best cooked just before serving, as it tends to go rubbery when cold.

SERVING SUGGESTION Serve with crusty wood-fired bread.

PREP + COOK TIME 35 MINUTES

1 TABLESPOON EXTRA VIRGIN OLIVE OIL

1.2KG (2½ POUNDS) WHOLE CLEANED BABY OCTOPUS

1 CLOVE GARLIC, SLICED THINLY

3 SHALLOTS (75G), SLICED THINLY

4 BABY EGGPLANTS (240G), SLICED THINLY

1 MEDIUM RED CAPSICUM (BELL PEPPER) (200G), SLICED THINLY

½ CUPS (125ML) DRY RED WINE

700G BOTTLED TOMATO PASTA SAUCE

⅔ CUP (160ML) WATER

¼ CUP (40G) BABY CAPERS

2 TABLESPOONS FRESH OREGANO LEAVES

1 Heat half of the oil in a large deep heavy-based frying pan. Cook octopus, in batches, until it just changes in colour and is tender. Cover to keep warm.

2 Heat remaining oil in same pan; cook garlic and shallot, stirring for 5 minutes or until shallot softens. Add eggplant and capsicum; cook, stirring, for 5 minutes or until vegetables are just tender.

3 Add wine, sauce, the water and octopus to pan; bring to the boil. Reduce heat to low-medium; simmer, covered, for 10 minutes or until sauce thickens slightly and octopus is tender. Stir in capers.

4 Serve octopus topped with oregano leaves.

The French diet

From accents and culture, to lifestyle and food, regional differences abound in France. In southern France, you couldn't be further from the butter-rich cuisine of the north west or the lard and sausage-laden dishes of the mountainous south east. Blessed by a sunny climate that brings long, hot, dry summers, France's Mediterranean areas, which include the region of Provence, are famous for almonds, olives, chickpeas, garlic, honey and stunning local fruit crops (figs, apricots, strawberries, cherries, melons). These all play a big part in the traditional diet, which is based on olive oil as the main fat and is particularly rich in fresh vegetables. Cooking meals from scratch using fresh local ingredients from local markets or growers, is key to the southern French way of life. All across France there's a genuine appreciation for food and the country's culinary reputation, that's instilled from a very young age. Conviviality and a pleasure in dining are at the core of the French attitude to food.

As well as the sun, the sea defines the South; a long coastline means there's a wealth of fish and seafood dishes. This is best seen in two of the region's most famous hearty soup-stews: bouillabaisse and bourride. Salt cod is used to make brandade, an appetiser based on garlicky, pureed potato. Anchovies, rich in omega-3 fats, flavour and enrich many dishes such as the onion tart pissaladiere and salade niçoise. So too does anchoiade, a potent condiment that's made by pounding anchovies with garlic. Snapper, red mullet, sea urchin, sea bass, prawns, mussels, lobsters, clams and squid are other fish favourites.

France's typical, everyday diet is relatively simple, with unprocessed, seasonal, full-fat foods such as meat, fish, grains, cheese, wine, vegetables and breads, at its core. Cooking techniques, commonly roasting, poaching, grilling, braising and sautéing, allow the ingredients to shine. Salads and other raw vegetable dishes are a big feature and a meal is likely to start with a selection of crudités (such as radish, witlof and artichokes) with an olive-based dip, or a rich, homemade aïoli. Garlic is used lavishly; aigo boulido, for instance, is a soup based on garlic. Pistou, a basil and garlic-based sauce, not unlike pesto, is spooned over soupe au pistou, a hearty stew of white beans, fresh vegetables and pasta. Aromatic herbs are used liberally to accentuate punchy flavours; not only do these taste wonderful, but they also have powerful antioxidant and other health benefits. Tomatoes are such a common thread through southern French cuisine that the term 'a la Provençal' signifies that a dish contains a fair amount of tomato. Eggplants, squash, zucchini, onion, artichokes and fennel are also crucial and are often served stuffed with rice and aromatics then baked, as a main course. Ratatouille is perhaps France's most renowned vegetable dish; it's a Provençal main, comprising lightly stewed tomato, eggplant, zucchini, onion and herbs.

Dessert is most likely to be fresh fruit, with cheese enjoyed as a separate course preceding it. Wine is another essential part of the diet and lifestyle. Not only is it thought that wine assists with digestion and can be good for your heart (in moderation!), but it's basic to the underlying tenet of leisurely enjoyment and sociability at the heart of French dining.

THE FRENCH LIFESTYLE

MEAL TIMES
The French tend not to snack: they stick to three meals a day and are fine with being a little hungry in between. Skipping meals is also not part of their dining regime.

LUNCH & DINNER
Lunch is more important than dinner, which tends to be a far lighter meal.

SOCIABILITY
In southern France, as in other parts of the Mediterranean, it's important to eat together; this includes work colleagues as well as families.

KIDS' FOOD
There's generally no special menu or separate meals for children – kids eat what adults are having. Salads, the cheese course... the whole nine yards.

WATER & WINE
Having water on the table is an essential part of dining, even when drinking wine.

PORTION CONTROL
The French generally are masters of small-portion dining. Even when they indulge in their famous patisserie or rich cakes, portion control is key.

roast salmon with fennel & apple salad

SERVES 10

As one of the richest food sources of omega-3 fatty acids, it is recommended we eat oily fish such as salmon at least twice a week for good brain function and heart health. This is not difficult to do at all when you serve it with this fresh, crisp salad. The sweet and sour combination of apple and fennel not only complement each other, but together also cut through the richness of the salmon.

TIPS Verjuice is an unfermented grape juice with a fresh lemony-vinegar flavour. It is available in major supermarkets, usually in the vinegar section. Salmon can also be cooked on a covered barbecue.

PREP + COOK TIME 1 HOUR 15 MINUTES (+ STANDING)

2.5KG (5-POUND) WHOLE SALMON, CLEANED, HEAD REMOVED

1 MEDIUM ONION (150G), SLICED THINLY

1 MEDIUM LEMON (140G), SLICED

4 FRESH BAY LEAVES

6 SPRIGS FRESH BASIL

2 TABLESPOONS EXTRA VIRGIN OLIVE OIL

1 CUP (250ML) VERJUICE

LEMON WEDGES, TO SERVE

FENNEL & APPLE SALAD

¼ CUP (40G) CURRANTS

¼ CUP (60ML) VERJUICE (SEE TIPS)

80G (2½ OUNCES) FRESH FLAT-LEAF PARSLEY STEMS

1 LARGE FENNEL BULB (550G)

2 SMALL FRESH APPLES (260G)

¼ CUP (60ML) EXTRA VIRGIN OLIVE OIL

1 Preheat oven to 200°C/400°F.

2 Wipe salmon cavity clean; season inside and out. Fill cavity with onion, lemon, bay leaves and basil. Secure opening with skewers.

3 Line a large oven tray with foil, then baking paper; brush paper with oil. Place salmon in the centre. Pour verjuice over salmon; fold foil and paper over salmon to enclose tightly.

4 Bake salmon for 50 minutes or until almost cooked through. Remove from oven; stand for 20 minutes.

5 Meanwhile, make fennel and apple salad.

6 Carefully peel away skin from salmon. Transfer salmon to a large platter. Remove skewers.

7 Strain cooking juices into a small saucepan; place over high heat until hot.

8 Top salmon with half the salad, drizzle with warm cooking juices. Serve salmon with remaining salad, reserved fennel fronds and lemon wedges.

FENNEL & APPLE SALAD Combine currants and verjuice in a small bowl. Cover; stand for 10 minutes or until required. Pick leaves from parsley; finely chop half the parsley stems, discard remaining stems. Reserve fronds from fennel. Thinly slice fennel using a mandoline or V-slicer. Peel and core apples; cut into matchsticks using a mandoline or V-slicer. Place currant mixture, parsley leaves, chopped parsley stems, apple, fennel and oil in a large bowl; toss gently to combine. Season to taste.

lamb shank & bean ragù

SERVES 4

French-trimmed lamb shanks have had the the upper ends of the bones trimmed slightly short and scraped (the point being to expose the cleaned bone), while the shank meat itself has been trimmed of excess fat, membrane and sinew. Shanks require long cooking to bring out their best taste and texture, and frenching them makes the end result more tender, less fatty and absolutely delicious.

TIPS Use a 400g can drained, rinsed cannellini beans and a 400g can drained, rinsed borlotti beans, instead of soaking and precooking dried beans, if you like; start the recipe at step 3.

SERVING SUGGESTION Serve with polenta or mashed potato.

PREP + COOK TIME 2 HOURS 30 MINUTES (+ STANDING)

YOU NEED TO START THIS RECIPE AT LEAST 8 HOURS AHEAD.

½ CUP (100G) DRIED HARICOT BEANS (SEE TIPS)

½ CUP (100G) DRIED BORLOTTI BEANS (SEE TIPS)

2 TABLESPOONS PLAIN (ALL-PURPOSE) FLOUR

8 FRENCH-TRIMMED LAMB SHANKS (1.6KG)

2 TABLESPOONS EXTRA VIRGIN OLIVE OIL

1 LARGE ONION (200G), CHOPPED FINELY

1 MEDIUM CARROT (120G), CHOPPED FINELY

1 STALK CELERY (150G), TRIMMED, CHOPPED FINELY

2 CLOVES GARLIC, CRUSHED

1 FRESH LONG RED CHILLI, CHOPPED FINELY

¼ CUP (60ML) BALSAMIC VINEGAR

400G (12½ OUNCES) CANNED CRUSHED TOMATOES

8 ANCHOVY FILLETS IN OIL

1 CINNAMON STICK

2 SPRIGS FRESH ROSEMARY

½ CUP (125ML) RED WINE

2 CUPS (500ML) WATER

¼ CUP COARSLEY CHOPPED FRESH FLAT-LEAF PARSLEY

1 Place dried beans in a large bowl, cover with cold water; soak 8 hours or overnight.

2 Drain soaked beans, rinse under cold water; drain. Place beans in a medium saucepan, cover with water; bring to the boil. Reduce heat to medium; cook for 15 minutes (beans will not be fully cooked at this stage). Drain.

3 Preheat oven to 180°C/350°F.

4 Place flour in a medium bowl; season. Toss lamb in flour; shake off excess. Heat half the oil in a large flameproof casserole dish over medium heat; cook lamb, in batches, turning, until browned all over. Remove from pan. Wipe pan clean if necessary.

5 Heat remaining oil in same pan over medium heat; cook onion, carrot, celery, garlic and chilli, stirring, for 5 minutes or until onion softens.

6 Return lamb to pan; add beans, vinegar, tomatoes, anchovies, cinnamon, rosemary, wine and the water. Bring to the boil; cover. Transfer to oven; cook, covered, for 1 hour, turning shanks halfway through cooking. Uncover; cook for a further 1 hour or until meat is almost falling off the bone.

7 Just before serving, sprinkle ragù with parsley.

greek vegetable pie with yellow split pea dip

SERVES 8

Although called a pie, this traditional Greek baked vegetable-and-herb-packed recipe is more like a frittata, as it contains no pastry.

TIPS Kefalotyri is a semi-firm greek sheep's or goat's milk cheese. The breadcrumbs are best made from bread that is about 3 days old. If you only have fresh bread, leave the slices on the bench for a few hours to dry out. Process bread, with or without crusts, until coarse crumbs form. Top sprinkled with fresh small mint leaves before serving, if you like.

PREP + COOK TIME 1 HOUR 15 MINUTES (+ STANDING & COOLING)

250G (8 OUNCES) ZUCCHINI, SLICED VERY THINLY

1 TEASPOON FINE SEA SALT

780G (1½ POUNDS) SILVER BEET (SWISS CHARD)

200G (6½ OUNCES) GREEN BEANS, TRIMMED

125G (4 OUNCES) GREEK FETTA, CRUMBLED

125G (4 OUNCES) KEFALOTYRI CHEESE (SEE TIPS) OR PARMESAN, GRATED COARSELY

¼ CUP CHOPPED FRESH FLAT-LEAF PARSLEY LEAVES

2 TABLESPOONS CHOPPED FRESH DILL

1 TABLESPOON CHOPPED FRESH MINT LEAVES

¾ CUP (50G) FRESH BREADCRUMBS (SEE TIPS)

6 EGGS, BEATEN LIGHTLY

¼ CUP (35G) SESAME SEEDS, TOASTED

1 TABLESPOON EXTRA VIRGIN OLIVE OIL

8 SMALL POCKET PITTAS, WARMED

LEMON WEDGES, TO SERVE

YELLOW SPLIT PEA DIP

1 CUP (200G) DRIED YELLOW SPLIT PEAS

1 SMALL ONION (80G), CHOPPED

4 CLOVES GARLIC, BRUISED

1 TEASPOON GROUND CUMIN

1 TEASPOON GROUND CORIANDER

⅓ CUP (80ML) EXTRA VIRGIN OLIVE OIL

¼ CUP (60ML) LEMON JUICE

1 Preheat oven to 180°C/350°F. Oil a 24cm (9½-inch) springform pan; line base with baking paper.

2 Combine zucchini and salt in a colander over a bowl; stand 30 minutes. Rinse zucchini under cold water; drain. Pat dry with paper towel. Trim stems from silver beet; discard stems. You will need 300g (9½ ounces) leaves.

3 Meanwhile, cook beans in a large saucepan of boiling water for 5 minutes or until tender. Remove beans with a slotted spoon, refresh in a bowl of iced water; drain well. Finely chop beans.

4 Add silver beet to water in pan, return to the boil; drain immediately. Refresh under cold running water; drain well. Squeeze silver beet to remove excess moisture; pat dry with paper towel. Finely chop silver beet.

5 Place zucchini, beans and silver beet in a large bowl with cheeses, herbs, breadcrumbs, egg, sesame seeds and oil; mix well to combine. Season. Spoon mixture into lined pan; smooth surface.

6 Bake pie for 35 minutes or until golden and set. Stand in pan for 15 minutes.

7 Meanwhile, make yellow split pea dip.

8 Serve pie warm or at room temperature with dip, pitta bread and lemon wedges.

YELLOW SPLIT PEA DIP Place split peas in a small saucepan with enough cold water to just cover; bring to the boil. Drain; rinse. Return peas to pan with onion and garlic, add enough cold water to cover by 6cm (2½ inches); bring to the boil. Reduce heat to medium; cook for 25 minutes or until peas are tender and beginning to collapse. Drain. Cool to room temperature. Process split pea mixture and spices until smooth. With motor operating, gradually add oil in a steady stream, then add juice in a steady stream. Season to taste. (Makes about 2½ cups)

roasted beef with salsa verde & panzanella salad

SERVES 8

TIPS You can roast the beef in a preheated covered barbecue over medium heat; the cooking time will be the same. It is best to use day-old bread in the panzanella, or you can toast the bread cubes first to dry them out a little.

PREP + COOK TIME 35 MINUTES (+ STANDING)

2 CLOVES GARLIC, CHOPPED

1 TABLESPOON FRESH THYME LEAVES

2 TABLESPOONS EXTRA VIRGIN OLIVE OIL

2 TABLESPOONS BALSAMIC VINEGAR

3KG (6-POUND) WHOLE RUMP OF BEEF

SALSA VERDE

¼ CUP CHOPPED FRESH FLAT-LEAF PARSLEY

¼ CUP CHOPPED FRESH BASIL

1 CLOVE GARLIC, CRUSHED

2 TEASPOONS BABY CAPERS

1 TEASPOON DIJON MUSTARD

¼ CUP (60ML) EXTRA VIRGIN OLIVE OIL

2 TEASPOONS RED WINE VINEGAR

PANZANELLA SALAD

3 MEDIUM RED CAPSICUMS (BELL PEPPERS) (600G)

3 MEDIUM YELLOW CAPSICUMS (BELL PEPPERS) (600G)

10 MEDIUM RIPE TOMATOES (1.5KG)

⅔ CUP (160ML) EXTRA VIRGIN OLIVE OIL

¼ CUP (60ML) RED WINE VINEGAR

1 LOAF CIABATTA BREAD (440G), CRUSTS REMOVED, CUT INTO 2CM (¾-INCH) PIECES

125G (4 OUNCES) BABY BLACK OLIVES

2 TABLESPOONS BABY CAPER

2 SHALLOTS (50G), SLICED THINLY

1 CUP TORN FRESH BASIL LEAVES

¼ CUP FRESH FLAT-LEAF PARSLEY LEAVES

1 Preheat oven to 200°C/400°F.

2 Combine garlic, thyme, oil and vinegar in a small bowl; rub all over beef. Stand at room temperature for 1 hour; season.

3 Place beef in a roasting pan; roast for 30 minutes for medium-rare or until cooked as desired. Stand, covered loosely with foil, for at least 15 minutes (or up to 30 minutes).

4 Meanwhile, make salsa verde, then panzanella salad.

5 Cut beef into thick slices; spoon over salsa verde. Serve with panzanella salad.

SALSA VERDE Combine herbs, garlic and capers in a small bowl; whisk in mustard, oil and vinegar until thickened. Season to taste.

PANZANELLA SALAD Preheat grill (broiler). Quarter capsicums; discard seeds and membrane. Place, skin-side up, on a large foil-lined oven tray. Place under grill for 10 minutes or until skin blisters and blackens. Cover with foil; stand for 10 minutes. When capsicum are cool enough to handle, peel away skins. Cut a small cross in the base of each tomato; plunge into boiling water, in batches, for 1 minute or until skin loosens. Immediately transfer to a bowl of iced water to cool. Drain and peel tomatoes; cut into wedges, discard seeds. Whisk oil and vinegar in a small bowl; season to taste. Ten minutes before serving, place capsicum, tomato, dressing and remaining ingredients in a large bowl; toss gently to combine.

seeded carrot & cabbage fillo pie
SERVES 6

Seeds and nuts are little nutritional powerhouses. Walnuts in particular offer an array of antioxidant and anti-inflammatory nutrients, as well as valuable monosaturated and omega-3 fatty acids. Roasting seeds and nuts amplifies their flavour and, if they're a little on the stale side, will freshen them up.

SERVING SUGGESTION
Serve with Greek-style yoghurt seasoned with freshly cracked black pepper, if you like.

PREP + COOK TIME 1 HOUR (+ COOLING)

½ CUP (125ML) EXTRA VIRGIN OLIVE OIL

1 LARGE LEEK (500G), WHITE PART ONLY, SLICED THINLY

3 CLOVES GARLIC, CRUSHED

2 TEASPOONS CARAWAY SEEDS

3 MEDIUM CARROTS (360G), GRATED COARSELY

375G (12 OUNCES) SAVOY CABBAGE, SHREDDED

⅓ CUP (55G) CURRANTS

⅓ CUP FINELY CHOPPED FRESH MINT

14 SHEETS FILLO PASTRY (210G)

SEED TOPPING

¼ CUP (50G) PEPITAS (PUMPKIN SEED KERNELS)

¼ CUP (35G) SLIVERED ALMONDS

¼ CUP (25G) COARSELY CHOPPED WALNUTS

1 TABLESPOON POPPY SEEDS

1 TABLESPOON SESAME SEEDS

HERB SALAD

1 LEBANESE CUCUMBER (130G)

½ CUP FRESH FLAT-LEAF PARSLEY LEAVES

½ CUP FRESH CURLY PARSLEY LEAVES

¼ CUP FRESH MINT LEAVES

¼ CUP FRESH DILL

2 GREEN ONIONS (SCALLIONS), SLICED THINLY

1 TABLESPOON RED WINE VINEGAR

2 TABLESPOONS EXTRA VIRGIN OLIVE OIL

1 Heat ⅓ cup of the oil in a large frying pan over medium heat; cook leek, garlic and caraway seeds for 5 minutes. Add carrot; cook for 3 minutes. Add cabbage; cook for a further 5 minutes or until vegetables are soft. Stir in currants and mint. Cool.
2 Make seed topping.
3 Preheat oven to 180°C/350°F.
4 Divide filling into seven portions. Brush one sheet of pastry with a little of the oil; top with a second sheet. Keep remaining sheets covered with baking paper topped with a clean, damp tea towel to prevent them from drying out. Place one portion of the filling lengthways, in a thin line, along pastry edge; roll pastry over filling. Starting at the centre of a 24cm (9½-inch) springform pan, carefully form the pastry roll, seam-side down, into a coil. Repeat with remaining pastry sheets, oil and filling, joining each roll to the end of the last one and coiling it around until the base of the pan is covered. Brush top with oil.
5 Bake fillo pie for 20 minutes. Cover pie evenly with seed topping; bake for a further 10 minutes or until golden.
6 Meanwhile, make herb salad.
7 Serve fillo pie with herb salad.
SEED TOPPING Combine ingredients in a small bowl.
HERB SALAD Using a vegetable peeler, peel cucumber into ribbons. Place cucumber in a medium bowl; add remaining ingredients; toss gently to combine. Season to taste.

lamb ragù moussaka

SERVES 8

Oven-baked casseroles are common in Greek cooking and moussaka is often considered the country's national dish. Here we've layered the eggplant with fall-apart slow-cooked lamb and cheesy sauce.

TIP Fresh breadcrumbs are best made from bread that is about three days old. If you only have fresh bread, leave the slices out on the bench for a few hours to dry out. Process bread, with or without crusts, until coarse crumbs form.

DO-AHEAD You can make the lamb ragù a day ahead. When lamb is cool enough to handle, shred the meat into pieces using two forks. Stir the shredded meat into the cooking sauce. Store in the refrigerator until ready to use. Reheat ragù as instructed in step 5. The lamb ragù also makes a rich, hearty sauce to serve with short pasta.

PREP + COOK TIME 5 HOURS

3 MEDIUM EGGPLANTS (960G)

OLIVE-OIL SPRAY

80G (2½ OUNCES) BUTTER, CHOPPED

½ CUP (75G) PLAIN (ALL-PURPOSE) FLOUR

1 LITRE (4 CUPS) MILK

1¼ CUPS (100G) FINELY GRATED PARMESAN

¾ CUP (50G) FRESH SOURDOUGH BREADCRUMBS
(SEE TIP)

2 TEASPOONS FINELY GRATED LEMON RIND

2 TEASPOONS FRESH THYME LEAVES

LAMB RAGÙ

2KG (4-POUND) BONELESS LEG OF LAMB

2 MEDIUM ONIONS (300G), CHOPPED COARSELY

4 CLOVES GARLIC, CHOPPED COARSELY

600G (1¼ POUNDS) CANNED CRUSHED TOMATOES

¼ CUP (70G) TOMATO PASTE

3 BAY LEAVES

½ CUP (125ML) RED WINE

1 TEASPOON GROUND CORIANDER

1 TEASPOON GROUND CUMIN

2 TABLESPOONS EXTRA VIRGIN OLIVE OIL

1 Make lamb ragù.

2 Preheat oven to 240°C/475°F.

3 Cut eggplants lengthways into medium-thick slices. Spray each side with olive-oil spray. Place on wire racks on oven trays; roast for 10 minutes or until soft and brown at edges. Remove from oven. Reduce oven to 200°C/400°F.

4 Meanwhile, melt butter in a medium saucepan over medium heat, add flour; cook, stirring until mixture bubbles. Gradually pour in milk, whisking continuously until mixture boils and thickens. Add ½ cup (40g) of the parmesan, stir until melted.

5 Remove lamb from roasting pan; shred meat. Place cooking sauce from pan in a large saucepan over low heat, add shredded meat; stir ragù until heated through. Season to taste.

6 Combine breadcrumbs, rind, thyme and remaining parmesan in a medium bowl.

7 Oil a 24cm x 32cm x 6.5cm (9½-inch x 12¾-inch x 2¾-inch), 3.5-litre (14-cup) capacity ovenproof dish. Place half the eggplant slices in the dish, then top with half the ragù and half the white sauce. Repeat layering. Sprinkle with breadcrumb mixture.

8 Bake moussaka for 35 minutes or until golden and heated through.

LAMB RAGÙ Preheat oven to 160°C/325°F. Trim excess fat from lamb, if necessary. Place onion, garlic, tomatoes, paste, bay leaves, and wine in a roasting pan. Combine spices in a small bowl. Rub oil over lamb, then spice mixture; place lamb on top of vegetable mixture in pan. Cover pan tightly with foil; roast lamb for 4 hours or until it is very tender. Discard bay leaves.

coq au vin

SERVES 4

Literally meaning 'rooster in wine', this is a quintessential French peasant dish. Braising slowly for hours was a favourite way of transforming tougher, less common meats (such as rooster) into a hearty, nourishing meal. Chicken has since replaced the rooster and it no longer requires such a long cooking time to develop the characteristic flavours.

TIP Serve this classic French braised chicken with mashed potato or toasted sourdough bread, if you like.

PREP + COOK TIME 1 HOUR 30 MINUTES

750G (1½ POUNDS) SPRING ONIONS

¼ CUP (60ML) EXTRA VIRGIN OLIVE OIL

4 RINDLESS BACON SLICES (390G),
    CHOPPED COARSELY

310G (10½ OUNCES) BUTTON MUSHROOMS

2 CLOVES GARLIC, CRUSHED

8 CHICKEN THIGH FILLETS (880G)

¼ CUP (35G) PLAIN (ALL-PURPOSE) FLOUR

2 CUPS (500ML) DRY RED WINE

1½ CUPS (375ML) CHICKEN STOCK

2 TABLESPOONS TOMATO PASTE

3 BAY LEAVES

4 SPRIGS FRESH THYME

2 SPRIGS FRESH ROSEMARY

1 Trim green ends from spring onions, leaving about 4cm (1½ inches) of stem attached; trim roots. Heat 1 tablespoon of oil in large heavy-based frying pan; cook onions, stirring, for 5 minutes or until browned all over; transfer to a large bowl.

2 Add bacon, mushrooms and garlic to pan. Cook, stirring, until bacon is crisp and mushrooms lightly browned; transfer to bowl with onions.

3 Coat chicken in flour; shake off excess. Heat remaining oil in same pan. Cook chicken, in batches, turning occasionally, for 8 minutes or until browned all over; drain on paper towel.

4 Return chicken, bacon mixture and onions to pan; add wine, stock, paste, bay leaves, thyme and rosemary. Bring to the boil; reduce heat to low, cook for 35 minutes or until chicken is tender and sauce has thickened slightly.

Sweets

whole orange semolina cake with rosemary syrup

SERVES 12

Semolina is a coarsely ground flour milled from the hardest part (endosperm) of the durum wheat grain and is commonly used making gnocchi, pasta and couscous. As it is a wheat product, it is not gluten-free, but is high in potassium, is digested more slowly than white flour and is fibre-rich. Here it imparts a rich, nutty flavour to the cake, kept extra moist with the aromatic syrup.

TIPS If you don't have a zester, simply peel the rind into wide strips with a vegetable peeler, then cut into thin strips. The cake is best made on the day of serving.

PREP + COOK TIME 2 HOURS 40 MINUTES (+ STANDING)

2 LARGE ORANGES (600G)

1 TEASPOON BAKING POWDER

6 EGGS

1 CUP (220G) CASTER (SUPERFINE) SUGAR

1 CUP (150G) FINE SEMOLINA

1¼ CUPS (150G) ALMOND MEAL

1½ TEASPOONS FINELY CHOPPED FRESH ROSEMARY

ROSEMARY SYRUP

2 LARGE ORANGES (600G)

½ CUP (110G) CASTER (SUPERFINE) SUGAR

½ CUP (125ML) WATER

1½ TABLESPOONS LEMON JUICE

2 TABLESPOONS ORANGE-FLAVOURED LIQUEUR

3 X 8CM (3¼-INCH) SPRIGS FRESH ROSEMARY

1 Place unpeeled oranges in a medium saucepan, cover with cold water; bring to the boil. Cook, covered, for 1½ hours or until oranges are tender; drain. Cool.

2 Preheat oven to 180°C/350°F. Grease a deep 22cm (9-inch) round cake pan; line base and side with baking paper.

3 Trim and discard ends from oranges. Halve oranges; discard seeds. Process orange, including rind, with baking powder until mixture is pulpy. Transfer to a large bowl.

4 Process eggs and sugar for 5 minutes or until thick and creamy. Stir egg mixture into orange mixture. Fold in semolina, almond meal and rosemary. Spread mixture into lined pan.

5 Bake cake for 1 hour or until a skewer inserted into the centre comes out clean; cover loosely with foil halfway during baking if over browning. Leave cake to cool in pan for 45 minutes. Transfer, top-side up, onto a cake plate.

6 Meanwhile, make rosemary syrup.

7 Spoon hot syrup over warm cake. Serve cake warm or at room temperature.

ROSEMARY SYRUP Remove rind from one orange into long thin strips with a zester. Using a vegetable peeler, peel a long continuous strip of rind from remaining orange. Place sugar, the water and juice in a small saucepan over low heat; stir, without boiling, until sugar dissolves. Add long strip of rind, bring to the boil; boil for 5 minutes or until syrup thickens. Remove from heat; stir in liqueur, rosemary and thin strips of rind.

pistachio, walnut & chocolate baklava

MAKES 36

Baklava is probably the most recognisable of all sweet Greek pastries, with its origins going all the way back to the Ottoman Empire. It is a rich, sticky dessert made of layers of fillo pasty filled with chopped nuts and held together with either a sugar syrup or honey. We've added dark chocolate to our version of baklava, to up the decadent level of this sweet treat, the perfect end to a good meal.

SERVING SUGGESTION
Serve with Greek-style yoghurt, sprinkled with finely grated or thinly sliced orange rind, if you like.

PREP + COOK TIME 1 HOUR 10 MINUTES (+ STANDING)

12 SHEETS FILLO PASTRY

120G (4 OUNCES) UNSALTED BUTTER, MELTED

2 TABLESPOONS FINELY CHOPPED PISTACHIOS

PISTACHIO & WALNUT FILLING

1½ CUPS (210G) PISTACHIOS

2 CUPS (200G) WALNUTS

200G (6 OUNCES) DARK (SEMI-SWEET) CHOCOLATE, CHOPPED COARSELY

⅓ CUP (75G) CASTER (SUPERFINE) SUGAR

2 TEASPOONS GROUND CINNAMON

1½ TABLESPOONS FINELY GRATED ORANGE RIND

HONEY SYRUP

1 MEDIUM ORANGE (240G)

1½ CUPS (330G) CASTER (SUPERFINE) SUGAR

1½ CUPS (375ML) WATER

½ CUP (175G) HONEY

⅓ CUP (80ML) ORANGE JUICE

1 Preheat oven to 190°C/375°F. Grease a 22cm x 40cm x 2.5cm (9-inch x 16-inch x 1-inch) oven tray; line with baking paper.

2 Make pistachio and walnut filling.

3 Layer three pastry sheets, brushing each with a little of the butter. Keep remaining sheets covered with baking paper and topped with a clean, damp tea towel to prevent drying out. Spread a quarter of the filling over pastry, leaving a 3cm (1¼-inch) border along both long sides. Starting at one long side, roll up pastry to form a log. Place log on oven tray, brush with butter. Repeat with remaining pastry, butter and filling.

4 Bake baklava for 20 minutes or until golden.

5 Meanwhile, make honey syrup.

6 Stand baklava on tray for 5 minutes to cool slightly. Using a small sharp knife, cut each log, on the diagonal, into nine 2cm (¾-inch) wide pieces in the tray. Pour hot syrup over baklava; stand for 3 hours or until syrup is absorbed. Serve topped with chopped pistachios.

PISTACHIO & WALNUT FILLING Spread pistachios and walnuts on an oven tray; roast in a 180°C/350°F oven for 5 minutes or until nuts are golden brown (stir nuts once during roasting for even cooking). Cool completely. Process nuts with remaining ingredients until finely chopped.

HONEY SYRUP Remove rind from orange into long thin strips with a zester. Stir rind, sugar, the water and honey in a small saucepan, over medium heat, without boiling, until sugar dissolves. Bring to a simmer; cook for 10 minutes or until thickened slightly. Stir in juice.

raspberry ricotta cheesecake
SERVES 8

The inclusion of ricotta in this cheesecake makes the filling lighter and less rich than the traditional cream-cheese based dessert. Amaretti are Italian biscuits made from almonds, often refered to as Italian macaroons, which legend has were created to welcome a visiting cardinal to the town of Saronno. The recipe for the biscuits was supposedly kept as a family secret over many generations.

TIPS Amaretti biscuits are available from delicatessens and supermarkets. You can use thawed frozen raspberries for the raspberry sauce, if you like. Depending on the design of the springform pan, clip the base in upside down so the base is level; this makes it easier to remove the cheesecake.

PREP + COOK TIME 1 HOUR 30 MINUTES (+ REFRIGERATION & COOLING)

200G (6½ OUNCES) AMARETTI BISCUITS (SEE TIPS)

2 TABLESPOONS CASTER (SUPERFINE) SUGAR

75G (2½ OUNCES) UNSALTED BUTTER, MELTED

125G (4 OUNCES) RASPBERRIES

2 TABLESPOONS ICING (CONFECTIONERS') SUGAR

2 TABLESPOONS WATER

125G (4 OUNCES) RASPBERRIES, EXTRA

2 TEASPOONS ICING (CONFECTIONERS') SUGAR, EXTRA

RASPBERRY RICOTTA FILLING

500G (1 POUND) CREAM CHEESE

300G (9½ OUNCES) RICOTTA

1 CUP (220G) CASTER (SUPERFINE) SUGAR

⅓ CUP (80ML) MILK

3 EGGS

125G (4 OUNCES) RASPBERRIES

1 Grease a 20cm (8-inch) springform pan; line base and side with baking paper.

2 Process biscuits and caster sugar until fine crumbs form. With motor operating, gradually add butter until well combined. Press biscuit mixture over base of lined pan using the back of a spoon. Place pan on an oven tray; refrigerate for 30 minutes.

3 Preheat oven to 150°C/300°F.

4 Make raspberry ricotta filling; pour filling into lined pan.

5 Bake for 50 minutes or until cheesecake is cooked around the edge and slightly wobbly in the middle. Turn oven off; cool cheesecake in oven for 1 hour with the door ajar. (The top of the cheesecake may crack slightly on cooling.) Refrigerate for 4 hours or overnight, until firm.

6 Process raspberries, icing sugar and the water until pureed. Strain through a sieve into a small bowl. Spread some puree over cheesecake, top with extra raspberries; dust with extra icing sugar. Serve with remaining puree.

RASPBERRY RICOTTA FILLING Process cheeses, sugar and milk until smooth. Add eggs; process until combined. Transfer mixture to a large bowl; fold in raspberries.

216

melt 'n' mix strawberry yoghurt cake

SERVES 8

Mediterranean desserts sometimes have the reputation for being overly fussy (though meals are often concluded simply with fresh fruits, some sharp cheese and a night-time tipple). Here we have a moist and nutty cake that requires no more than one bowl to prepare, so there is no excuse not to indulge in a freshly-baked cake for dessert.

TIP Cake and macerated strawberries are best made on day of serving.

PREP + COOK TIME 1 HOUR 15 MINUTES (+ COOLING)

2½ CUPS (375G) SELF-RAISING FLOUR

250G (8 OUNCES) STRAWBERRIES,
    CHOPPED COARSELY

1 CUP (220G) GOLDEN CASTER (SUPERFINE) SUGAR

1 TEASPOON VANILLA BEAN PASTE

2 EGGS, BEATEN LIGHTLY

½ CUP (140G) GREEK-STYLE YOGHURT

125G (4 OUNCES) UNSALTED BUTTER, MELTED

½ CUP (40G) FLAKED ALMONDS

ICING (CONFECTIONERS') SUGAR, FOR DUSTING

1 CUP (280G) GREEK-STYLE YOGHURT, EXTRA

MACERATED STRAWBERRIES

250G (8 OUNCES) STRAWBERRIES, SLICED

1 TABLESPOON LEMON JUICE

1 TABLESPOON GOLDEN CASTER (SUPERFINE)
    SUGAR

1 Preheat oven to 180°C/350°F. Grease a 22cm (9-inch) springform pan; line base and side with baking paper.

2 Sift flour into a large bowl; stir in strawberries, sugar, vanilla paste, egg, yoghurt and butter until just combined. Spoon mixture into pan; smooth the surface. Sprinkle with almonds.

3 Bake cake for 50 minutes or until a skewer inserted into the centre comes out clean; cover loosely with foil halfway though baking if almonds are over browning. Leave cake in pan for 10 minutes. Release ring; transfer cake to a wire rack to cool.

4 Meanwhile, make macerated strawberries.

5 Top cake with macerated strawberries and dust with icing sugar; serve with extra yoghurt.

MACERATED STRAWBERRIES Combine ingredients in a small bowl; stand for 20 minutes.

honey & vanilla custard pots with fillo crunch

SERVES 4

Fillo comes from the Greek word for leaf, referring to its thin, paper-like texture. This unleavened dough is mainly used for making pastries, both sweet and savoury, by layering many sheets of fillo brushed with olive oil or butter, which when baked, results in a very crumbly, delicate structure. Here the fillo is used as a crunchy element to contrast the smooth, silky honey custard.

TIP Swap figs with ripe strawberries, raspberries or your favourite stone fruit, if preferred.

PREP + COOK TIME 40 MINUTES (+ REFRIGERATION & COOLING)

¼ CUP (90G) HONEY

2 CUPS (500ML) MILK

1 VANILLA BEAN, SPLIT LENGTHWAYS

2 TABLESPOONS CUSTARD POWDER

1 TABLESPOON BROWN SUGAR

1 SHEET FILLO PASTRY

OLIVE-OIL SPRAY

2 TABLESPOONS FINELY CHOPPED UNSALTED
    PISTACHIOS

1 TABLESPOON HONEY, EXTRA, WARMED

4 MEDIUM FRESH FIGS (240G), QUARTERED (SEE TIP)

1 Place honey, milk and vanilla bean in a medium saucepan over medium heat; bring to a simmer.
2 Whisk custard powder and sugar in a medium heatproof bowl until combined. Gradually whisk warm milk mixture into custard mixture; return to pan. Bring to the boil, whisking constantly, until mixture boils and thickens. Discard vanilla bean.
3 Pour mixture into four 1 cup (250ml) dishes. Refrigerate for 2 hours or until chilled and firm.
4 Meanwhile, preheat oven to 180°C/350°F. Line an oven tray with baking paper.
5 Place pastry sheet on a work surface; spray with oil. Sprinkle two-thirds of the pistachios over pastry. Fold pastry in half crossways; brush with extra honey, sprinkle with remaining pistachios. Bake for 8 minutes or until golden and crisp; cool. Break into pieces.
6 Serve custards topped with figs and fillo crunch, drizzled with a little more honey, if you like.

dark chocolate & ricotta mousse

SERVES 6

The hard and fast rule for chocolate is that the higher percentage of cocoa, the better it is for you. Quality dark chocolate is rich in fibre, iron and magnesium, and is a great source of antioxidants. While of course you shouldn't be eating large quantities of chocolate, especially in one sitting, as it high in sugar and kilojoules, a bit of dark chocolate in your diet is great sweet treat.

TIPS Fresh pomegranate seeds are sometimes found in the fridge section of supermarkets or good greengrocers. If they're not available, see page 30 for instructions on how to remove them. Alternatively, top each serving with fresh cherries instead.

PREP + COOK TIME 20 MINUTES (+ COOLING)

¼ CUP (90G) HONEY

1 TABLESPOON DUTCH-PROCESSED COCOA

2 TABLESPOONS WATER

½ TEASPOON VANILLA EXTRACT

200G (6½ OUNCES) DARK CHOCOLATE (70% COCOA), CHOPPED COARSELY

8 FRESH DATES (160G), PITTED

½ CUP (125ML) MILK

2 CUPS (480G) SOFT RICOTTA

2 TABLESPOONS POMEGRANATE SEEDS (SEE TIPS)

2 TABLESPOONS CHOPPED PISTACHIOS

1 Stir honey, cocoa, the water and extract in a small saucepan over medium heat; bring to the boil. Cool.

2 Place chocolate in a small heatproof bowl over a small saucepan of simmering water (don't let the water touch the base of the bowl); stir until melted and smooth.

3 Process dates and milk until dates are finely chopped. Add ricotta; process until smooth. Add melted chocolate; process until well combined.

4 Spoon mousse evenly into six ¾ cup (180ml) serving glasses. Spoon cocoa syrup on mousse; top with pomegranate seeds and pistachios.

roasted fig & yoghurt ice-cream
SERVES 8

This is more of a frozen yoghurt, so it is less creamy than traditional ice-cream. Lower in fat than cream, this also makes it a healthier choice. Greek-style yoghurt is rich in probiotics, which are live bacteria and yeasts that are good for your health, especially your digestive system. The probiotic found in yoghurt is known as lactobacillus, which helps breaks down lactose.

TIPS Stand ice-cream at room temperature for 10 minutes to soften slightly before serving. If you have an ice-cream machine, this mixture can be churned following the manufacturer's instructions. Store leftover ice-cream in the freezer for up to 1 month.

PREP + COOK TIME 45 MINUTES (+ COOLING & FREEZING)

6 LARGE RIPE FIGS (480G), TORN IN HALF

¾ CUP (165G) BROWN SUGAR

2 TEASPOONS FINELY GRATED ORANGE RIND

⅓ CUP (80ML) FRESHLY SQUEEZED ORANGE JUICE

3 CUPS (840G) GREEK-STYLE YOGHURT

⅔ CUP (160G) CRÈME FRAÎCHE

⅓ CUP (115G) HONEY, PLUS EXTRA TO SERVE

6 RIPE FIGS (240G), EXTRA, HALVED

1 Preheat oven to 220°C/425°F. Grease and line an oven tray with baking paper.

2 Place figs, sugar, rind and juice on tray; toss to combine. Spread figs on lined tray in one layer, cut-side up; roast for 15 minutes or until tender and bubbling. Cool for 10 minutes.

3 Grease a 2-litre (8-cup) loaf pan; line base and sides with baking paper; extending the paper 5cm (2 inches) over long sides.

4 Combine yoghurt, crème fraîche and honey in a large bowl; gently fold in caramelised figs and the fig roasting juices. Spoon mixture into lined pan. Freeze for 4 hours or until partially frozen.

5 Remove from freezer. Coarsely chop mixture; place in a large food processor bowl, pulse to break up the ice crystals. Return to pan. Freeze for 4 hours or until firm.

6 Serve ice-cream topped with extra figs; drizzle with extra honey.

citrus yoghurt cups

SERVES 4

In the dark cold months of winter, the only bright spot is the copious ripe, juicy citrus fruits that come into season. While it is well known that citrus are an excellent source of vitamin C, which helps boost your immune system in the cold and flu season, they also possess other health benefits, such as the antioxidant-rich red grapefruit helping to lower 'bad' LDL cholesterol as well as triglyceride levels.

TIP For orange strips, use a vegetable peeler to peel wide strips and avoid taking off too much of the white pith with the rind, as it is bitter.

DO-AHEAD The syrup can be made 4 hours ahead and combined with the citrus; refrigerate until needed.

PREP + COOK TIME 45 MINUTES

1 VANILLA BEAN

⅓ CUP (75G) CASTER (SUPERFINE) SUGAR

½ CUP (125ML) WATER

6 WIDE STRIPS ORANGE RIND (SEE TIP)

1 TABLESPOON ORANGE JUICE

2 MEDIUM MANDARINS (200G), PEELED, SLICED HORIZONTALLY

1 MEDIUM RUBY GRAPEFRUIT (350G), PEELED, SEGMENTED

3 CUPS (840G) GREEK-STYLE YOGHURT

SMALL FRESH MINT LEAVES, TO SERVE

1 Split vanilla bean in half lengthways; scrape seeds into a small saucepan. Add vanilla pod, sugar, the water and rind to pan; bring to the boil. Reduce heat to low; cook for 6 minutes or until syrup has thickened slightly. Cool. Discard vanilla pod; stir in juice.

2 Combine mandarin and grapefruit slices and sugar syrup in a medium bowl.

3 Spoon yoghurt into four 1¼ cup (310ml) serving glasses. Top with citrus mixture and mint.

honey-baked peaches & grapes with sweet ricotta
SERVES 4

There is no more straight-forward dessert than baked fruit, where their bright, sweet flavours are amplified to become a delicious warming dish which is healthy to boot. Accompanied here with a sweetened ricotta, you could also serve the fruit with ice-cream, crème fraîche or creamy Greek-style yoghurt. Or use the fruit and syrup as a topper for a plain cake, for a show-stopping dessert.

TIPS Use a combination of yellow and white peaches, if you like, or swap plums for peaches. This dish can be served for brunch or dessert. It also travels well, so is a great picnic basket addition. Pack the ricotta and fruit separately; keep ricotta cold.

PREP + COOK TIME 40 MINUTES

4 LARGE PEACHES (880G), STONES REMOVED, QUARTERED (SEE TIPS)

400G (12½ OUNCES) RED GRAPES, HALVED, SEEDS REMOVED

1 TABLESPOON HONEY

4 SPRIGS FRESH THYME, PLUS EXTRA TO SERVE

1½ CUPS (360G) FIRM RICOTTA

2 TABLESPOONS CASTER (SUPERFINE) SUGAR

½ TEASPOON FINELY GRATED ORANGE RIND, PLUS EXTRA TO SERVE

1 Preheat oven to 200°C/400°F. Line an oven tray with baking paper.
2 Place peaches and grapes on tray; drizzle with honey and top with thyme. Bake for 25 minutes or until tender and syrupy.
3 Meanwhile, process ricotta, sugar and rind until smooth.
4 Serve baked fruit and any cooking juices with ricotta mixture, topped with extra orange rind and fresh thyme.

baked ricotta pudding with orange syrup & cherries

SERVES 4

Honey has been collected by humans from ancient times, and in the absence of sugar, was used as a sweetener in many traditional desserts in the Mediterranean region. In fact the earliest recording of honey havesting is in an 8,000-years-old cave painting in Valencia, Spain, which depicts two figures using a ladder or series of ropes to gather the sweet liquid from high bee hives.

TIP You can use a mixture of yellow and red cherries and halve them, if you like.

PREP + COOK TIME 1 HOUR (+ COOLING & REFRIGERATION)

900G (1¾ POUNDS) RICOTTA

4 EGGS

½ CUP (175G) HONEY

¾ TEASPOON GROUND CINNAMON

2 TEASPOONS FINELY GRATED ORANGE RIND

100G (3 OUNCES) FRESH CHERRIES, SEEDED (SEE TIP)

2 TABLESPOONS COARSELY CHOPPED PISTACHIOS

ORANGE SYRUP

1 LARGE ORANGE (300G)

½ CUP (175G) HONEY

100ML WATER

1 CINNAMON STICK

½ TEASPOON FRESH THYME LEAVES

1 Preheat oven to 180°C/350°F. Grease a 1 litre (4 cup) ovenproof dish.

2 Process ricotta, eggs, honey, cinnamon and rind until smooth. Pour mixture evenly into dish.

3 Bake pudding for 30 minutes or until centre is just firm to touch. Cool to room temperature. Refrigerate for 1 hour or until cold.

4 Meanwhile, make orange syrup.

5 Serve pudding topped with cherries, orange syrup, and pistachios.

ORANGE SYRUP Finely grate rind from orange; squeeze juice, you will need ¼ cup (60ml) orange juice. Combine rind, juice and remaining ingredients in a small saucepan; bring to the boil. Reduce heat to low; cook for 10 minutes or until syrupy. Refrigerate for 1 hour or until cold.

glossary

ALLSPICE also known as pimento or jamaican pepper; so-named because it tastes like a combination of nutmeg, cumin, clove and cinnamon. Available whole or ground.

ALMONDS

blanched brown skins removed.

flaked paper-thin slices of blanched or natural almonds.

meal powdered to a coarse flour-like texture.

natural almond kernels with the brown skin on.

slivered small pieces cut lengthways.

ANCHOVIES small oily fish. Anchovy fillets are preserved and packed in oil or salt in small cans or jars, and are strong in flavour. Fresh anchovies are much milder in flavour.

BACON also known as bacon slices or rashers.

BAKING POWDER a raising agent consisting mainly of two parts cream of tartar to one part bicarbonate of soda (baking soda).

BARLEY a nutritious grain used in soups and stews. Hulled barley, the least processed, is high in fibre. Pearl barley has had the husk removed then been steamed and polished so that only the "pearl" of the original grain remains, much the same as white rice.

BASIL, SWEET the most common type of basil; used extensively in Italian dishes and one of the main ingredients in pesto.

BAY LEAVES aromatic leaves from the bay tree available fresh or dried; adds a strong, slightly peppery flavour.

BEANS

borlotti also called roman beans or pink beans, can be eaten fresh or dried. Interchangeable with pinto beans due to their similarity in appearance – pale pink or beige with dark red streaks.

broad (fava) available dried, fresh, canned and frozen. Fresh should be peeled twice (discarding the outer long green pod and the beige-green tough inner shell); frozen beans have had their pods removed but the beige shell still needs removal.

butter cans labelled butter beans are, in fact, cannellini beans. Confusingly butter is also another name for lima beans (dried and canned); a large beige bean having a mealy texture and mild taste.

cannellini a small white bean similar in appearance and flavour to other white beans (great northern, navy or haricot), all of which can be substituted for the other. Available dried or canned.

green also known as french or string beans (although the tough string they once had has generally been bred out of them), this long thin fresh bean is consumed in its entirety once cooked.

haricot the haricot bean family includes navy beans and cannellini. All are mild-flavoured white beans which can be interchangeable.

white a generic term we use for canned or dried cannellini, haricot, navy or great northern beans belonging to the same family, phaseolus vulgaris.

BEEF

gravy boneless stewing beef from shin; slow-cooked, imbues stocks, soups and stews with a gelatine richness. Cut crossways, with bone in, is osso buco.

minced also known as ground beef.

rump boneless tender cut taken from the upper part of the hindquarter. Cut into steaks, good for barbecuing; as one piece, great as a roast.

BEETROOT (BEETS) firm, round root vegetable.

BREADCRUMBS

fresh bread, usually white, processed into crumbs.

packaged prepared fine-textured but crunchy white breadcrumbs; good for coating foods that are to be fried.

stale crumbs made by grating, blending or processing 1- or 2-day-old bread.

BURGHUL also called bulghur wheat; hulled steamed wheat kernels that, once dried, are crushed into various sized grains. Used in Middle Eastern dishes such as felafel, kibbeh and tabbouleh. Is not the same as cracked wheat.

BUTTER we use salted butter unless stated otherwise; 125g is equal to 1 stick (4 ounces).

CAPERBERRIES olive-sized fruit formed after the buds of the caper bush have flowered; they are usually sold pickled in a vinegar brine with stalks intact.

CAPERS grey-green buds of a warm climate shrub (usually Mediterranean); sold either dried and salted or pickled in a vinegar brine; tiny young ones, called baby capers, are also available both in brine or dried in salt. Their pungent taste adds piquancy to a tapenade, sauces and condiments.

CAPSICUM (BELL PEPPER) also called pepper. Discard seeds and membranes before use.

CARAWAY SEEDS the small, half-moon-shaped dried seed from a member of the parsley family; adds a sharp anise flavour when used in both sweet and savoury dishes.

CAVOLO NERO also known as tuscan cabbage. Has long, narrow, wrinkled leaves and a rich and astringent, mild cabbage flavour. It doesn't lose its volume like silver beet or spinach when cooked, but it does need longer cooking.

CELERIAC (CELERY ROOT) tuberous root with knobbly brown skin, white flesh and a celery-like flavour. Keep peeled celeriac in acidulated water to stop it discolouring.

CHEESE

bocconcini from the diminutive of "boccone", meaning mouthful in Italian; walnut-sized, baby mozzarella, a delicate, semi-soft, white cheese traditionally made from buffalo milk. Sold fresh, it spoils rapidly so will only keep, refrigerated in brine, for 1 or 2 days at the most.

cream commonly called philadelphia or philly; a soft cow-milk cheese, its fat content ranges from 14 to 33%.

fetta Greek in origin; a crumbly textured goat- or sheep-milk cheese having a sharp, salty taste. Ripened and stored in salted whey.

goat's made from goat's milk, has an earthy, strong taste; available in both soft and firm textures, in various shapes and sizes, and sometimes rolled in ash or herbs.

haloumi a firm, cream-coloured sheep-milk cheese matured in brine; haloumi can be grilled or fried without breaking down. Should be eaten while still warm as it becomes rubbery on cooling.

mascarpone an Italian fresh cultured-cream product made in much the same way as yoghurt. Whiteish to creamy yellow in colour, with a buttery-rich, luscious texture. Soft, creamy and spreadable, it is used in Italian desserts and as an accompaniment to fresh fruit.

mozzarella soft, spun-curd cheese; originating in southern Italy where it was traditionally made from water-buffalo milk. Now generally made from cow's milk, it is the most popular pizza cheese because of its low melting point and elasticity when heated.

parmesan also called parmigiano; is a hard, grainy cow-milk cheese originating in Italy. Reggiano is the best variety.

ricotta a soft, sweet, moist, white cow-milk cheese with a low fat content and a slightly grainy texture. The name roughly translates as 'cooked again' and refers to ricotta's manufacture from a whey that is itself a by-product of other cheese making.

CHICKPEAS (GARBANZO BEANS) an irregularly round, sandy-coloured legume. Firm texture even after cooking; available canned or dried (reconstitute for several hours in water before use).

CHILLI

flakes also sold as crushed chilli; dehydrated deep-red extremely fine slices and whole seeds.

long available both fresh and dried; a generic term used for any moderately hot, thin, long (6-8cm/2¼-3¼ inch) chilli.

CHIVES related to the onion and leek; has a subtle onion flavour. Used more for flavour than as an ingredient; chopped finely, they're good in sauces, dressings, omelettes or as a garnish.

CHOCOLATE, DARK (SEMI-SWEET) also known as luxury chocolate; made of a high percentage of cocoa liquor and cocoa butter, and little added sugar.

CINNAMON available both in the piece (called sticks or quills) and ground into powder; one of the world's most common spices, used universally as a sweet, fragrant flavouring for both sweet and savoury foods.

CORIANDER (CILANTRO) also known as pak chee or chinese parsley; a bright-green leafy herb with a pungent flavour. Used as an ingredient in a wide variety of cuisines. Both stems and roots of coriander are also used in cooking; wash well before using. Also available ground or as seeds; these should not be substituted for fresh as the tastes are completely different.

CORNICHON French for gherkin, a very small variety of cucumber. Pickled, they are a traditional accompaniment to pâté.

COUSCOUS a fine, grain-like cereal product made from semolina. A semolina flour and water dough is sieved then dehydrated to produce minuscule even-sized pellets of couscous; it is rehydrated by steaming or with the addition of a warm liquid and swells to three or four times its original size.

CREAM, POURING also called pure or fresh cream. It has no additives and contains a minimum fat content of 35%.

CRÈME FRAÎCHE a mature, naturally fermented cream (minimum fat content 35%) having a velvety texture and slightly tangy, nutty flavour.

CUMIN also known as zeera or comino; resembling caraway in size, cumin is the dried seed of a plant related to the parsley family. Its spicy, almost curry-like flavour is essential to the traditional foods of Mexico, India, North Africa and the Middle East. Available dried as seeds or ground. Black cumin seeds are smaller than standard cumin, and dark brown rather than true black; they are mistakenly confused with kalonji.

CURRANTS tiny, almost black raisins so-named after a grape variety that originated in Corinth, Greece.

CUSTARD POWDER instant mixture used to make pouring custard; similar to North American instant pudding mixes.

DILL also known as dill weed; used fresh or dried, in seed form or ground. Its anise/celery sweetness flavours the food of the Scandinavian countries, and Germany and Greece. Its feathery, frond-like fresh leaves are grassier and more subtle than the dried version or the seeds (which slightly resemble caraway in flavour).

DUKKAH an Egyptian specialty spice mixture made up of roasted nuts, seeds and an array of aromatic spices.

EGGPLANT also called aubergine. Ranging in size from tiny to very large and in colour from pale green to deep purple.

FENNEL also called finocchio or anise; a crunchy green vegetable slightly resembling celery that's eaten raw in salads; fried as an accompaniment; or used as an ingredient in soups and sauces. Also the name given to the dried seeds of the plant which have a stronger licorice flavour.

FILLO PASTRY paper-thin sheets of raw pastry; brush each sheet with oil or melted butter, stack in layers, then cut and fold as directed.

FLOUR

chickpea (besan) creamy yellow flour made from chickpeas; it is very nutritious.

plain (all-purpose) a general all-purpose wheat flour.

self-raising plain flour sifted with baking powder in the proportion of 1 cup flour to 2 teaspoons baking powder.

wholemeal also known as wholewheat flour; milled with the wheat germ so is higher in fibre and more nutritional than plain flour.

FREEKEH is cracked roasted green wheat and can be found in some larger supermarkets, health food and specialty food stores.

GINGER

fresh also called green or root ginger; the thick gnarled root of a tropical plant. Can be kept, peeled, covered with dry sherry in a jar and refrigerated, or frozen in an airtight container.

ground also called powdered ginger; used as a flavouring in baking but cannot be substituted for fresh ginger.

GRAPEVINE LEAVES from early spring, fresh grapevine leaves can be found in most specialist greengrocers. Alternatively, cryovac-packages containing about 60 leaves in brine can be found in Middle-Eastern food shops and some delicatessens; these must be rinsed and dried before using.

JUNIPER BERRIES dried berries of an evergreen tree; it is the main flavouring ingredient in gin.

LAMB

backstrap also known as eye of loin; the larger fillet from a row of loin chops or cutlets. Tender, best cooked rapidly: barbecued or pan-fried.

cutlet small, tender rib chop; sometimes sold french-trimmed, with all the fat and gristle at the narrow end of the bone removed.

leg cut from the hindquarter; can be boned, butterflied, rolled and tied, or cut into dice.

minced ground lamb.

shoulder large, tasty piece having much connective tissue so is best pot-roasted or braised. Makes the best mince.

LENTILS (red, brown, yellow) dried pulses often identified by and named after their colour. Eaten by cultures all over the world, most famously perhaps in the dhals of India, lentils have high food value.

French-style green lentils related to the famous french lentils du puy; these green-blue, tiny lentils have a nutty, earthy flavour and a hardy nature that allows them to be rapidly cooked without disintegrating.

MAYONNAISE, WHOLE-EGG commercial mayonnaise of high quality made with whole eggs and labelled as such; some prepared mayonnaises substitute emulsifiers such to achieve the same thick and creamy consistency but never achieve the same rich flavour.

MILK we use full-cream homogenised milk unless otherwise specified.

buttermilk originally the term given to the slightly sour liquid left after butter was churned from cream, today it is made from no-fat or low-fat milk to which specific bacterial cultures have been added. Despite its name, it is actually low in fat.

MIXED SPICE a classic spice mixture generally containing caraway, allspice, coriander, cumin, nutmeg and ginger, although cinnamon and other spices can be added. It is used with fruit and in cakes.

MUSLIN inexpensive, undyed, finely woven cotton fabric called for in cooking to strain stocks and sauces.

MUSTARD, DIJON also called french. Pale brown, creamy, distinctively flavoured, fairly mild French mustard.

NUTMEG a strong and pungent spice ground from the dried nut of an evergreen tree native to Indonesia. Usually found ground but the flavour is more intense from a whole nut, available from spice shops, so it's best to grate your own. Used most often in baking and milk-based desserts, but also works nicely in savoury dishes. Found in mixed spice mixtures.

OIL

cooking spray we use a cholesterol-free cooking spray made from canola oil.

olive made from ripened olives. Extra virgin and virgin olive oil are the first and second press, respectively, of the olives; "light" refers to the taste of the oil, not fat levels.

ONIONS

green (scallions) also called, incorrectly, shallot; an immature onion picked before the bulb has formed, has a long, bright-green stalk.

red also known as spanish, red spanish or bermuda onion; a sweet-flavoured, large, purple-red onion.

spring crisp, narrow green-leafed tops and a round sweet white bulb larger than green onions.

OREGANO a herb, also known as wild marjoram; has a woody stalk and clumps of tiny, dark-green leaves. Has a pungent, peppery flavour.

PAPRIKA ground dried sweet red capsicum (bell pepper); there are many grades and types available, including sweet, hot, mild and smoked.

PASTRY SHEETS ready-rolled packaged sheets of frozen puff and shortcrust pastry, available from supermarkets.

PEPITAS (PUMPKIN SEED KERNELS) are the pale green kernels of dried pumpkin seeds; available plain or salted.

PINE NUTS not a nut but a small, cream-coloured kernel from pine cones. Toast before use to bring out their flavour.

PISTACHIOS green, delicately flavoured nuts inside hard off-white shells. Available salted or unsalted in their shells; you can also get them shelled.

POLENTA also known as cornmeal; a flour-like cereal made of ground corn (maize). Also the name of the dish made from it.

POMEGRANATE dark-red, leathery-skinned fruit about the size of an orange filled with hundreds of seeds, each wrapped in an edible lucent-crimson pulp with a unique tangy sweet-sour flavour.

molasses not to be confused with pomegranate syrup or grenadine (used in cocktails); pomegranate molasses is thicker, browner, and more concentrated in flavour — tart and sharp, slightly sweet and fruity. Buy from Middle Eastern food stores or specialty food shops.

POPPY SEEDS small, dried, bluish-grey seeds of the poppy plant, with a crunchy texture and a nutty flavour. Can be purchased whole or ground.

QUINOA pronounced keen-wa; is cooked and eaten as a grain, but is in fact a seed. It has a delicate, slightly nutty taste and chewy texture.

RADICCHIO a red-leafed Italian chicory with a refreshing bitter taste that's eaten raw and grilled. Comes in varieties named after their places of origin, such as round-headed Verona or long-headed Treviso.

RICE

black high in nutritional value; the grain has a similar amount of fibre to brown rice and, like brown rice, has a mild, nutty taste.

brown retains the high-fibre, nutritious bran coating that's removed from white rice when hulled. It takes longer to cook than white rice and has a chewier texture.

ROCKET (ARUGULA) also called rugula and rucola; peppery green leaf eaten raw in salads or used in cooking. Baby rocket leaves are smaller and less peppery.

SAFFRON available ground or in strands; imparts a yellow-orange colour to food once infused. The quality can vary greatly; the best is the most expensive spice in the world.

SEAFOOD

calamari also known as squid; a type of mollusc. To clean calamari, gently pull the head and entrails away from the body, then remove and discard the clear quill. Cut the tentacles from the head just below the eyes, then remove the beak. Gently pull away the outer membrane from the hood. Cut into smaller pieces, if desired.

clams also called vongole; we use a small ridge-shelled variety of this bivalve mollusc.

fish fillets, firm white blue eye, bream, flathead, snapper, ling, swordfish, whiting, jewfish or sea perch are all good choices. Check for small pieces of bone and use tweezers to remove them.

mussels should only be bought from a reliable fish market: they must be tightly closed when bought, indicating they are alive. Before cooking, scrub shells with a strong brush and remove the beards; disgard any that are open before cooking, or smell off. Varieties include black and green-lip.

octopus usually tenderised before you buy them; both octopus and squid require either long slow cooking (for large molluscs) or quick cooking over high heat (for small molluscs) – anything in between will make the octopus tough and rubbery.

prawns (shrimp) varieties include, school, king, royal red, sydney harbour, tiger. Can be bought uncooked (green) or cooked, with or without shells.

salmon red-pink firm flesh with few bones; moist delicate flavour.

tuna reddish, firm flesh; slightly dry. Varieties include bluefin, yellowfin, skipjack or albacore; substitute with swordfish.

SEMOLINA coarsely ground flour milled from durum wheat; the flour used in making gnocchi, pasta and couscous.

SESAME SEEDS black and white are the most common of this small oval seed, however there are also red and brown varieties. The seeds are used as an ingredient and as a condiment.

SUGAR

brown very soft, finely granulated sugar retaining molasses for its characteristic colour and flavour.

caster (superfine) finely granulated table sugar.

icing (confectioners') also called powdered sugar; pulverised granulated sugar crushed with a little cornflour (cornstarch).

SUMAC a purple-red, astringent spice ground from berries growing on shrubs flourishing wild around the Mediterranean; adds a tart, lemony flavour to food. Available from supermarkets.

SUNFLOWER SEEDS grey-green, slightly soft, oily kernels; a nutritious snack.

TAHINI a rich, sesame-seed paste, used in most Middle-Eastern cuisines, especially Lebanese, in dips and sauces.

TURMERIC also called kamin; is a rhizome related to galangal and ginger. Must be grated or pounded to release its acrid aroma and pungent flavour. Known for the golden colour it imparts, fresh turmeric can be substituted with the more commonly found dried powder.

VANILLA

bean dried, long, thin pod from a tropical golden orchid; the minuscule black seeds inside the bean are used to impart a luscious vanilla flavour in baking and desserts. A bean can be used three or four times.

extract made by extracting the flavour from the vanilla bean pod; pods are soaked, usually in alcohol, to capture the authentic flavour.

paste made from vanilla pods and contains real seeds. Is highly concentrated – 1 teaspoon replaces a whole vanilla pod.

VINEGAR

apple cider made from fermented apples.

balsamic originally from Modena, Italy, there are now many balsamic vinegars on the market. Quality can be determined up to a point by price; use the most expensive sparingly.

sherry natural vinegar aged in oak according to the traditional Spanish system; a mellow wine vinegar named for its colour.

wine based on red or white wine.

WATERCRESS one of the cress family, a large group of peppery greens. Highly perishable, so must be used as soon as possible after purchase.

YEAST (dried and fresh), a raising agent used in dough making. Granular (7g sachets) and fresh compressed (20g blocks) yeast can almost always be substituted one for the other when yeast is called for.

YOGHURT, GREEK-STYLE plain yoghurt that has been strained in a cloth (muslin) to remove the whey and to give it a creamy consistency.

ZA'ATAR a blend of whole roasted sesame seeds, sumac and crushed dried herbs such as wild marjoram and thyme, its content is largely determined by the individual maker.

conversion chart

MEASURES

One Australian metric measuring cup holds approximately 250ml; one Australian metric tablespoon holds 20ml; one Australian metric teaspoon holds 5ml. The difference between one country's measuring cups and another's is within a two- or three-teaspoon variance, and will not affect your cooking results. North America, New Zealand and the United Kingdom use a 15ml tablespoon. All cup and spoon measurements are level.

The most accurate way of measuring dry ingredients is to weigh them.

When measuring liquids, use a clear glass or plastic jug with the metric markings. We use large eggs with an average weight of 60g.

DRY MEASURES

metric	imperial
15g	½oz
30g	1oz
60g	2oz
90g	3oz
125g	4oz (¼lb)
155g	5oz
185g	6oz
220g	7oz
250g	8oz (½lb)
280g	9oz
315g	10oz
345g	11oz
375g	12oz (¾lb)
410g	13oz
440g	14oz
470g	15oz
500g	16oz (1lb)
750g	24oz (1½lb)
1kg	32oz (2lb)

LIQUID MEASURES

metric	imperial
30ml	1 fluid oz
60ml	2 fluid oz
100ml	3 fluid oz
125ml	4 fluid oz
150ml	5 fluid oz
190ml	6 fluid oz
250ml	8 fluid oz
300ml	10 fluid oz
500ml	16 fluid oz
600ml	20 fluid oz
1000ml (1 litre)	1¾ pints

LENGTH MEASURES

metric	imperial
3mm	⅛in
6mm	¼in
1cm	½in
2cm	¾in
2.5cm	1in
5cm	2in
6cm	2½in
8cm	3in
10cm	4in
13cm	5in
15cm	6in
18cm	7in
20cm	8in
22cm	9in
25cm	10in
28cm	11in
30cm	12in (1ft)

OVEN TEMPERATURES

The oven temperatures in this book are for conventional ovens; if you have a fan-forced oven, decrease the temperature by 10-20 degrees.

	°C (Celsius)	°F (Fahrenheit)
Very slow	120	250
Slow	150	300
Moderately slow	160	325
Moderate	180	350
Moderately hot	200	400
Hot	220	425
Very hot	240	475

Index